I0002362

MASTERING REGEX WITH PYTHON

Search, Match, and Manipulate Text

THOMPSON CARTER

All rights reserved

No part of this book may be reproduced, distributed, or transmitted in any form or by any means without the prior written permission of the publisher, except in the case of brief quotations embodied in critical reviews and certain other noncommercial uses permitted by copyright law.

TABLE OF CONTENTS

Introduction

Mastering Regex with Python: Search, Match, and Manipulate Text

In today's world of data-driven decision-making, managing and manipulating data efficiently is more important than ever. Whether you're working with large datasets, automating web scraping tasks, processing natural language, or validating user inputs, regular expressions (regex) have proven to be an indispensable tool. But despite their power, regex remains one of the most misunderstood and underutilized features in programming. This book, "Mastering Regex with Python: Search, Match, and Manipulate Text," aims to change that by providing a clear, structured, and comprehensive guide to mastering regular expressions using Python.

What This Book Offers

Regular expressions are, at their core, a language used for searching, matching, and manipulating text in highly specific ways. They allow you to create patterns that can efficiently identify, extract, and modify text, making them an essential tool for a range of tasks—from simple data cleaning to more complex text analysis. But regex can be intimidating. The syntax is dense, the behavior can sometimes seem unpredictable, and even experienced developers often find themselves re-learning how to craft patterns for new problems. This book addresses those challenges head-on, offering readers a clear, jargon-free approach to understanding and utilizing regex in Python.

"Mastering Regex with Python" is designed for a wide range of audiences. Whether you're a beginner programmer, a data analyst looking to clean messy datasets, a developer working with large volumes of text data, or even someone interested in the advanced applications of regex, this book will provide the tools, techniques, and examples you need to tackle regex problems with confidence.

Through 29 carefully structured chapters, you will learn how to:

1. **Understand the Basics of Regex:** Get to grips with regex syntax and functionality, starting with simple patterns and building up to more complex constructs. You'll learn how to use Python's re library to solve everyday problems.

2. **Apply Regex for Real-World Tasks:** With hands-on examples, you'll see how regex is used to search, extract, and manipulate text. Whether you're scraping web pages, cleaning data, or processing logs, you will see regex in action across a variety of use cases.

3. **Tackle Advanced Regex Topics:** Explore the more advanced capabilities of regex such as lookaheads, backreferences, and recursion, which are essential for working with nested or dynamic data. You'll also dive into

performance optimization and strategies for writing efficient regex.

4. **Master Practical Applications:** Regex isn't just theoretical—it's an incredibly powerful tool for tackling real-world challenges. We'll show you how to use regex for tasks such as validating user inputs, automating text replacements, parsing HTML/XML, and even performing data cleaning and transformation.

5. **Refine Your Regex Skills with Best Practices:** The book closes with a focus on best practices. Learn how to write clean, maintainable, and efficient regex patterns, debug issues effectively, and future-proof your regex knowledge by keeping up with emerging trends in text processing.

Why This Book?

Regex is used everywhere—across programming languages, in text editors, search engines, databases, and even in artificial intelligence (AI) systems. It's a tool that's indispensable for many practical tasks, such as:

- **Data Analysis:** Parsing logs, extracting patterns from datasets, and performing text-based analysis are all tasks where regex excels.

- **Web Scraping:** Regex can be combined with Python libraries like BeautifulSoup and Requests to extract structured data from unstructured web pages.

- **Natural Language Processing (NLP):** From tokenization to text cleaning, regex helps prepare text data for deeper analysis, such as sentiment analysis or machine learning applications.

- **Software Development:** From validation to parsing code and testing, regex plays a pivotal role in the development lifecycle.

- **Automation and AI:** As the automation landscape grows, regex is used in tools that analyze and transform vast amounts of text data, helping power intelligent systems.

However, the true power of regex comes when it is mastered—not just in its syntax but also in its practical application. Regex allows you to write code that can efficiently process data and make decisions based on complex textual patterns. With this book, you will gain the knowledge and confidence to wield regex as an invaluable tool in your development toolkit.

Real-World Examples

Throughout this book, you will encounter real-world examples that demonstrate how regex is applied to solve specific problems. For instance:

- **Validating user inputs:** Using regex to validate email addresses, phone numbers, and other user data to ensure they adhere to a specific format.

- **Extracting data from logs:** Using regex to parse and analyze log files from servers, systems, and applications.

- **Cleaning messy data:** Using regex for tasks such as removing unwanted characters, handling missing values, or standardizing text fields in messy datasets.

- **Scraping websites:** Regular expressions allow you to scrape specific data (such as product prices, stock quotes, etc.) from HTML pages efficiently.

- **Parsing HTML/XML:** With regex, you'll learn how to extract meaningful information from structured data formats, such as scraping metadata from web pages.

Each chapter is crafted to provide you with the knowledge and tools you need to solve these problems in an intuitive, step-by-step manner.

Who This Book is For

This book is designed for anyone interested in learning regex with Python, whether you're:

- **A beginner programmer** who is just starting out with Python and needs an accessible introduction to regex.

- **A data analyst** who wants to clean and manipulate data from text files, logs, or datasets.
- **A developer** looking to streamline tasks like validation, parsing, or automation with Python.
- **A data scientist** interested in preprocessing text for natural language processing (NLP) or machine learning tasks.
- **A seasoned coder** who wants to sharpen their regex skills and discover advanced techniques.

While the book starts with basic concepts and examples, it gradually advances to complex regex patterns, optimization strategies, and practical use cases that will appeal to experienced developers and data scientists alike.

What You Will Gain from This Book

By the end of this book, you will:

- **Master regex syntax and patterns** and understand the underlying logic behind regular expressions.
- Be able to **implement regex in a variety of real-world scenarios**, from data cleaning to web scraping to software development.
- **Write efficient, optimized regex** that can handle large datasets or complex tasks without unnecessary complexity or performance hits.

- Understand **advanced techniques** like backreferences, recursion, and lookaheads/behind, which are often necessary for solving more challenging problems.
- Be prepared to tackle **future trends** in regex applications, especially in automation, AI, and machine learning contexts.

Regex may seem daunting at first, but once you get the hang of it, you'll find that it's an incredibly powerful and versatile tool. In this book, we will guide you through the complexities of regex with clarity and hands-on examples to help you achieve mastery. By the end of this book, you'll have a deep understanding of regex in Python and be well-equipped to tackle a wide range of text processing challenges.

Let's Get Started

Ready to master regex with Python? Let's dive in and start exploring the world of regular expressions. The tools and techniques you'll learn here will not only enhance your programming skills but also empower you to solve real-world problems in data processing, analysis, and automation.

Chapter 1: Introduction to Regex and Python

What Are Regular Expressions (Regex)?

Regular expressions (regex) are sequences of characters that define a search pattern. These patterns are primarily used to match, find, or manipulate text in a string. They serve as a powerful tool for working with text-based data, helping automate repetitive tasks like searching, parsing, and data cleaning.

At their core, regex allows you to define patterns that can match various text sequences. For example:

- Searching for email addresses in a document.
- Validating phone numbers or dates in a string.
- Extracting specific patterns like ZIP codes, URLs, or hashtags.

Regex is not limited to programming languages like Python; it is a universal tool used in a wide range of technologies and tools, including text editors, command-line utilities, and web development frameworks.

Why Regex is a Powerful Tool for Text Processing

1. **Precision and Flexibility:** Regex gives you control over the exact text pattern you're looking for. Whether it's a simple

match like finding all occurrences of the word "python" or more complex patterns like validating email addresses or phone numbers, regex offers the flexibility to do it all. For example:

- ○ **Simple Match**: Finding all occurrences of a word.
- ○ **Complex Match**: Extracting all dates in a certain format (e.g., dd/mm/yyyy).

2. **Efficiency:** Regex allows you to perform text manipulations and searches with a single command, avoiding the need to write long loops or conditional statements. It is highly efficient for processing large datasets or documents where a simple match could take a lot of time manually.

3. **Pattern-Based Searches:** Regex can perform searches based on patterns rather than exact matches. This means you can easily find patterns such as email addresses, credit card numbers, or specific words regardless of their location in the text.

4. **Text Replacement:** Regex isn't just for matching text; you can also use it to replace text based on specific patterns. For example, replacing all email addresses in a document with a placeholder or formatting text in a standardized way.

Python's Built-In Regex Library: re

In Python, regex functionality is provided by the built-in re library. This library allows you to compile regular expressions, search through text, and manipulate strings based on the patterns you define.

The re library provides several important functions for working with regex:

- re.match(): Matches a regex pattern at the beginning of a string.
- re.search(): Searches the entire string for the first match of the pattern.
- re.findall(): Returns all non-overlapping matches of the pattern in a string as a list.
- re.sub(): Replaces parts of a string that match a regex pattern with a specified replacement.
- re.split(): Splits a string into a list at each occurrence of the pattern.

Example:

python

```python
import re

# Example 1: Search for a word in a string
pattern = r'python'
text = "I love programming in Python."

match = re.search(pattern, text)
if match:
    print("Found:", match.group())
else:
    print("Not found.")
```

Output:

makefile

Found: Python

Real-World Examples: How Regex is Used in Searching and Cleaning Data

1. **Searching for Specific Patterns:** Imagine you're working with a large text dataset, and you need to extract all email addresses. Regex provides a concise way to define the pattern for email addresses and quickly find all occurrences.

    Example:

    python

    ```
    text = "Contact us at support@example.com or sales@company.com"
    pattern = r'\b[A-Za-z0-9._%+-]+@[A-Za-z0-9.-]+\.[A-Z|a-z]{2,7}\b'

    emails = re.findall(pattern, text)
    print(emails)
    ```
    Output:

    css

    ```
    ['support@example.com', 'sales@company.com']
    ```

2. **Data Cleaning:** Regex is extremely useful for cleaning data. For instance, you might have a dataset containing phone numbers, but they could be formatted inconsistently (e.g.,

some with parentheses, others with dashes). With regex, you can standardize all phone numbers into a single format.

Example:

python

```
phone_numbers = ["(123) 456-7890", "123-456-7890", "456.789.0123"]
pattern = r'\D'  # Remove non-digit characters
cleaned_numbers = [re.sub(pattern, "", number) for number in phone_numbers]
print(cleaned_numbers)
```
Output:

css

```
['1234567890', '1234567890', '4567890123']
```

3. **Validating Inputs:** Regex is also crucial for input validation, such as ensuring that users enter valid email addresses, phone numbers, or postal codes. By defining the proper regex pattern, you can easily validate data before processing it further.

Example (email validation):

python

```
email = "example@domain.com"
pattern = r'^[a-zA-Z0-9_.+-]+@[a-zA-Z0-9-]+\.[a-zA-Z0-9-.]+$'
```

```
if re.match(pattern, email):
    print("Valid email")
else:
    print("Invalid email")
```

Output:

Valid email

Why This Chapter is Important

By the end of this chapter, you should have a solid understanding of what regex is, why it is an essential tool for text manipulation, and how Python's re library helps you use regex to search, match, and manipulate text effectively. This foundational knowledge will serve as the basis for the more advanced regex topics and real-world applications covered in later chapters.

In the following chapters, we will dive deeper into the specific regex patterns, syntax, and techniques that allow you to handle increasingly complex tasks, from data extraction and cleaning to pattern matching and text formatting.

This chapter introduces regex as a powerful tool in Python, with practical examples tailored to the everyday tasks faced by programmers and data analysts.

Chapter 2: Getting Started with Python and Regex

Setting Up Your Python Environment for Regex

Before diving into the world of regular expressions, it's important to ensure that you have the right environment set up for working with regex in Python. Python's built-in re library makes working with regular expressions simple and efficient. Fortunately, you don't need to install any additional libraries since re comes pre-installed with Python.

1. **Installing Python:**

   o If you haven't already installed Python, head to python.org and download the latest version for your operating system.

   o After installation, verify that it was successful by typing python --version (or python3 --version on some systems) in your terminal or command prompt.

2. **Creating Your First Python File:**

   o Open a text editor or an Integrated Development Environment (IDE) like VS Code, PyCharm, or Jupyter Notebooks.

   o Create a new Python file, for example regex_example.py, to start working on your regex scripts.

3. **Importing the re Library:**

   o   In Python, regular expressions are handled by the re module, so the first step in working with regex is to import this module. Here's how you can do it:

python

import re

The re module provides all the functions needed to perform operations like searching, matching, and replacing text using regex patterns.

Overview of Python's re Library

The re library contains a set of functions to allow you to search, match, and manipulate text patterns. Here are some key functions from the re module that you'll be using frequently:

- **re.match()**: Checks if the regular expression matches the beginning of the string.
- **re.search()**: Scans the entire string to find the first match of the pattern.
- **re.findall()**: Returns all non-overlapping matches of the pattern in the string.
- **re.sub()**: Replaces occurrences of the regex pattern with a specified string.
- **re.split()**: Splits the string at each match of the regex pattern.

The following code snippet demonstrates how to use some of these functions:

python

```
import re

# Sample string
text = "The price of the product is $45.99."

# Match a pattern
match = re.search(r'\$\d+\.\d{2}', text)
if match:
    print("Price found:", match.group())  # Output: $45.99
```

In the example above:

- \$\d+\.\d{2} is the regex pattern that matches a dollar sign (\$), followed by one or more digits (\d+), then a period (\.), and exactly two digits after the decimal point (\d{2}).
- match.group() returns the matched string.

First Steps: Simple Regex Patterns

Now that we've set up the environment and explored the re module, let's dive into creating our first regex pattern. At its core, regex allows us to define patterns for text matching.

Here are a few simple regex concepts and patterns you'll encounter frequently:

1. **Literal Characters**: These are simply the characters you want to match in the string. For example, to find the word "apple" in a text, you can use the literal string r'apple'.

2. **Metacharacters**: These are special characters that have a predefined meaning in regex. For example:

   o . (dot) matches any character except a newline.

   o ^ anchors the match at the beginning of the string.

   o $ anchors the match at the end of the string.

   o \d matches any digit (0-9).

   o \w matches any word character (letters, digits, and underscores).

   o \s matches any whitespace character (spaces, tabs, newlines).

Example of a simple regex:

python

```
import re

# Check if 'apple' is present in the text
text = "I have an apple."
match = re.search(r'apple', text)
if match:
    print("Found:", match.group())  # Output: Found: apple
```

3. **Quantifiers**: These specify how many times a character or group should appear in the match. For example:

- o * (zero or more)

- o + (one or more)

- o {n,m} (between n and m times)

Example with quantifiers:

python

import re

```
# Check for one or more digits
text = "The cost is 100 dollars."
match = re.search(r'\d+', text)  # Matches one or more digits
if match:
    print("Found:", match.group())  # Output: Found: 100
```

Real-World Example: Searching for Keywords in Text Files

Let's walk through a real-world scenario where regex can be used to search for keywords in a text file. Imagine you have a log file containing records of financial transactions, and you need to extract specific keywords such as "failure", "error", or "overdue".

Steps:

1. Open the text file.
2. Use regex patterns to find the keywords.
3. Extract the matching lines or words.

Here's an example of how this can be done in Python:

python

```python
import re

# Sample log data (in practice, this would be read from a file)
log_data = """
2023-01-01 Transaction Successful
2023-01-02 Transaction Failed: Insufficient funds
2023-01-03 Error: Invalid account number
2023-01-04 Payment Overdue: Contact support
"""

# Pattern to search for keywords 'failure', 'error', or 'overdue'
pattern = r'(failure|error|overdue)'

# Searching the log data for the pattern
matches = re.findall(pattern, log_data, re.IGNORECASE)

# Display matched keywords
if matches:
    print("Found the following issues in the log:")
    for match in matches:
        print(match)
else:
    print("No issues found.")
```

Output:

bash

```
Found the following issues in the log:
Failed
```

Error

Overdue

In this example:

- re.findall() is used to search through the log data for any of the keywords "failure", "error", or "overdue", regardless of case (re.IGNORECASE).
- The regex pattern (failure|error|overdue) matches any of the keywords within the parentheses, separated by the pipe symbol (|), which means "or."

In this chapter, you were introduced to the basics of Python's regex capabilities, including the use of the re library, fundamental regex syntax, and a real-world application of regex in text searching. As you continue to explore regular expressions in Python, you'll see how versatile and efficient regex can be for a wide range of text processing tasks.

In the next chapter, we will dive deeper into regex patterns and explore more complex use cases for text manipulation.

Chapter 3: Understanding Regex Syntax

Regular expressions (regex) are made up of various components, each with its own specific purpose. The syntax of regex can seem daunting at first, but with some practice, you will quickly become familiar with how to construct powerful patterns to search, match, and manipulate text. In this chapter, we'll break down the fundamental building blocks of regex syntax, covering literal characters, meta-characters, special symbols, and anchors. We'll also explore a real-world example of how regex can be used to match phone numbers in various formats.

Basic Syntax: Literal Characters, Meta-characters, and Special Symbols

1. **Literal Characters**:
   - A **literal character** is any character that appears exactly as it is in the string. For example, the pattern cat will match the exact sequence "cat" in a string.
   - Literal characters are the simplest form of regex patterns. If you want to match a specific sequence of characters, you can just type them directly into the regex pattern.
   - **Example**:

     python

```
import re
pattern = "dog"
text = "I have a dog."
match = re.search(pattern, text)
if match:
    print("Found:", match.group())
```

2. **Meta-characters**:

   o **Meta-characters** are special characters that have specific meanings in regex. These characters are not matched literally but are used to create more complex and flexible search patterns.

   o Some common meta-characters include:

   - **Dot (.)**: Matches any single character except a newline (\n).

   - **Asterisk (*)**: Matches 0 or more repetitions of the preceding element.

   - **Plus (+)**: Matches 1 or more repetitions of the preceding element.

   - **Question mark (?)**: Matches 0 or 1 repetition of the preceding element.

   o **Example**:

   python

```
pattern = "a.*b"  # Matches any string that starts with "a" and
ends with "b"
text = "a quick brown fox jumps over the lazy b"
```

```
match = re.search(pattern, text)
if match:
    print("Found:", match.group())
```

3. **Special Symbols**:

   o **Escape character (\)**: Some characters in regex have special meanings, like the dot (.) or parentheses (). If you want to match these characters literally, you need to **escape** them using a backslash (\).

   o For example, to match a period (.), use the pattern \\. in the regex.

   o **Example**:

   python

```
pattern = r"\."
text = "Hello. How are you?"
match = re.search(pattern, text)
if match:
    print("Found a period.")
```

Understanding Anchors: ^, $, \b, \B

Anchors are special regex symbols that help you specify **where** in the text you want to make a match. Anchors match a position, rather than a specific character.

1. **Caret (^)**:

- o The ^ anchor matches the **start** of a string. It's used when you want to ensure that a pattern only matches if it appears at the beginning of the string.
- o **Example**:

python

```
pattern = "^Hello"
text = "Hello, world!"
match = re.match(pattern, text)
if match:
    print("Found:", match.group())
```

2. **Dollar Sign ($)**:

- o The $ anchor matches the **end** of a string. It ensures that the pattern only matches if it appears at the end of the string.
- o **Example**:

python

```
pattern = "world!$"
text = "Hello, world!"
match = re.search(pattern, text)
if match:
    print("Found:", match.group())
```

3. **Word Boundary (\b)**:

o The \b symbol matches a **word boundary**, which is the position where a word starts or ends. It helps in matching whole words.

o For example, \bcat\b will match the word "cat" but not "catalog" or "scattered".

o **Example**:

python

```
pattern = r"\bcat\b"
text = "I have a cat."
match = re.search(pattern, text)
if match:
    print("Found:", match.group())
```

4. **Non-word Boundary (\B)**:

o The \B symbol matches a **non-word boundary**. This is used when you want to match positions that are **not** word boundaries.

o For example, \Bcat\B will match the "cat" in "scattered" but will not match the "cat" in "I have a cat."

o **Example**:

python

```
pattern = r"\Bcat\B"
text = "scattered"
```

MASTERING REGEX WITH PYTHON

```
match = re.search(pattern, text)
if match:
    print("Found:", match.group())
```

Real-world Example: Matching Phone Numbers in Varied Formats

Let's apply what we've learned so far by creating a regex pattern to match phone numbers in multiple formats. Phone numbers can appear in various ways depending on country, format, and separators (e.g., dashes, spaces, parentheses).

Here's an example of how you can use regex to match phone numbers in different formats like:

- (123) 456-7890
- 123-456-7890
- 123 456 7890
- 123.456.7890

1. **Regex Pattern**: We will build a regex pattern that allows us to match these different formats.

python

import re

# Regex to match different phone number formats
pattern = r"\(?\d{3}\)?[-.\s]?\d{3}[-.\s]?\d{4}"

```
# Test data with various phone number formats
texts = [
    "(123) 456-7890",
    "123-456-7890",
    "123 456 7890",
    "123.456.7890",
    "Invalid phone number"
]

for text in texts:
    match = re.search(pattern, text)
    if match:
        print(f"Found phone number: {match.group()}")
    else:
        print("No phone number found.")
```

2. **Explanation**:

   o \(?: Matches an optional opening parenthesis.

   o \d{3}: Matches exactly three digits.

   o \)?: Matches an optional closing parenthesis.

   o [-.\s]?: Matches an optional separator which could be a dash, period, or space.

   o \d{3} and \d{4}: Matches three digits followed by four digits (the second and third parts of the phone number).

This pattern matches phone numbers in all four formats and ignores invalid formats.

3. **Output**:

yaml

Found phone number: (123) 456-7890
Found phone number: 123-456-7890
Found phone number: 123 456 7890
Found phone number: 123.456.7890
No phone number found.

In this chapter, we've introduced the fundamental syntax of regular expressions. We've learned how to:

- Work with literal characters, meta-characters, and special symbols.
- Use anchors to match specific positions in a string.
- Build a regex pattern to match phone numbers in various formats.

By understanding and practicing these basic building blocks, you're now equipped to tackle more complex text processing tasks in Python. In the following chapters, we'll explore more advanced regex patterns and techniques for efficiently searching, matching, and manipulating text data.

Chapter 4: Working with Python's re Functions

Python's re library provides a suite of powerful functions that allow you to search, match, and manipulate strings using regular expressions. These functions are the core tools for applying regex patterns to text data. In this chapter, we will introduce and explore the key functions in the re library: re.match(), re.search(), re.findall(), and re.sub(). We will go through the functionality of each function with examples and a real-world use case of extracting email addresses from a text document.

1. re.match() – Matching at the Beginning

- **Definition**: The re.match() function attempts to match a pattern at the **start** of a string. If the pattern matches from the beginning, it returns a match object; otherwise, it returns None.
- **Syntax**:

  python

  re.match(pattern, string)

  - **pattern**: The regex pattern to search for.
  - **string**: The string to search through.
- **Example**:

python

```
import re
pattern = r"\d{3}"  # Match 3 digits
text = "123abc"
result = re.match(pattern, text)
print(result.group())  # Output: 123
```

In this example, re.match() looks for three digits at the start of the string. Since the string begins with "123", it matches successfully.

- **Limitations**: re.match() only returns a match if the pattern occurs **at the beginning** of the string. For other occurrences in the string, use re.search() (covered later).

2. *re.search() – Searching Anywhere in the String*

- **Definition**: The re.search() function scans the entire string for the first occurrence of the pattern. It returns a match object if found; otherwise, it returns None.
- **Syntax**:

python

```
re.search(pattern, string)
```

- o **pattern**: The regex pattern to search for.
- o **string**: The string to search through.
- **Example**:

python

```
import re
pattern = r"\d{3}"  # Match 3 digits
text = "abc123xyz"
result = re.search(pattern, text)
print(result.group())  # Output: 123
```

Here, re.search() looks through the string "abc123xyz" for the first occurrence of 3 consecutive digits and successfully matches "123".

- **When to Use**: Use re.search() when you need to find a match anywhere within the string, not just at the start.

3. re.findall() – Finding All Matches

- **Definition**: The re.findall() function finds **all** non-overlapping matches of a pattern in a string and returns them as a list of strings. It's useful when you need to extract multiple occurrences of a pattern.

- **Syntax**:

python

```
re.findall(pattern, string)
```

   o **pattern**: The regex pattern to search for.
   o **string**: The string to search through.

- **Example**:

python

```
import re
pattern = r"\d+"  # Match one or more digits
text = "The numbers are 123, 456, and 789."
result = re.findall(pattern, text)
print(result)  # Output: ['123', '456', '789']
```

In this case, re.findall() extracts all the numbers from the string and returns them as a list.

- **When to Use**: Use re.findall() when you need to capture multiple occurrences of a pattern, such as extracting multiple phone numbers or email addresses from a document.

4. re.sub() – Substituting Text

- **Definition**: The re.sub() function allows you to **replace** occurrences of a pattern with a specified replacement string. It returns the modified string.
- **Syntax**:

python

```
re.sub(pattern, replacement, string)
```

  - o **pattern**: The regex pattern to search for.
  - o **replacement**: The string to replace the matched text.
  - o **string**: The string to search through.
- **Example**:

python

```
import re
pattern = r"\d+"  # Match one or more digits
replacement = "[number]"
text = "The order numbers are 123 and 456."
result = re.sub(pattern, replacement, text)
print(result)  # Output: The order numbers are [number] and [number].
```

In this example, re.sub() replaces all digit sequences in the string with "[number]".

- **When to Use**: Use re.sub() when you need to modify or clean up text by replacing patterns with a new value. This function is especially useful for sanitizing data or formatting strings.

Real-World Example: Extracting Email Addresses from a Text Document

In this section, we'll use Python's re functions to extract email addresses from a text document. Email addresses follow a relatively consistent pattern and can be matched using regex.

Task: Extract all email addresses from a given text.

1. **Regex Pattern for Email Address**: A simple regex pattern for matching email addresses is:

regex

r"[a-zA-Z0-9._%+-]+@[a-zA-Z0-9.-]+\.[a-zA-Z]{2,}"

- o [a-zA-Z0-9._%+-]+: Matches the username part of the email.
- o @: Matches the @ symbol.
- o [a-zA-Z0-9.-]+: Matches the domain name part of the email.
- o \.[a-zA-Z]{2,}: Matches the top-level domain (e.g., .com, .org).

2. **Python Code**:

python

import re

```
# Sample text containing email addresses
text = """
Please contact john.doe@example.com for more information.
You can also reach support@mywebsite.org for assistance.
Send an email to admin123@company.co for technical issues.
"""

# Regex pattern for matching email addresses
pattern = r"[a-zA-Z0-9._%+-]+@[a-zA-Z0-9.-]+\.[a-zA-Z]{2,}"

# Using re.findall() to extract all email addresses
emails = re.findall(pattern, text)
```

```
# Output the list of emails
print(emails)
```

3. **Output**:

python

['john.doe@example.com', 'support@mywebsite.org', 'admin123@company.co']

In this example, the re.findall() function is used to search for all email addresses in the text, and it successfully extracts them into a list.

In this chapter, we've explored the key functions in Python's re library, including re.match(), re.search(), re.findall(), and re.sub(). These functions are the building blocks of working with regular expressions in Python, allowing you to search, extract, and modify text data. We also demonstrated how to apply these functions in real-world scenarios, such as extracting email addresses from a document. Mastery of these functions will enable you to tackle a wide range of text processing tasks in Python with ease.

Chapter 5: Character Classes and Ranges

In regular expressions, character classes are essential tools for specifying sets of characters that can appear in a string at a particular position. Character classes allow you to match a wide range of characters in a flexible and concise way, without having to explicitly list all possible characters. This chapter will cover the basics of character classes and ranges, and how you can use them in Python to extract or validate text efficiently.

We'll also explore how character sets can help you extract data in real-world scenarios, such as pulling numeric data from product descriptions.

---

1. What Are Character Classes?

A **character class** is a set of characters enclosed in square brackets ([]). It allows you to match any one of the characters in that set. For example:

- [abc] matches either an a, b, or c.
- [1-9] matches any digit from 1 to 9.

Character classes are a powerful feature in regex because they allow for more concise and flexible patterns. Let's take a look at some of the most commonly used character classes:

- **\d**: Matches any digit (equivalent to [0-9]).

- **\w**: Matches any alphanumeric character (letters and digits) and underscore (_).

- **\s**: Matches any whitespace character (spaces, tabs, line breaks).

- **.**: Matches any character except a newline.

These shorthand classes simplify regex patterns and can make your code more readable.

---

2. Ranges in Regex

A **range** is a shorthand for specifying a series of characters. It is used inside square brackets to define a span of characters. A few examples:

- **[a-z]**: Matches any lowercase letter from a to z.

- **[A-Z]**: Matches any uppercase letter from A to Z.

- **[0-9]**: Matches any digit from 0 to 9.

Ranges are extremely useful for matching groups of characters without having to list each one individually.

For example:

- [A-Za-z] will match any uppercase or lowercase letter.

- [0-9]{3} will match exactly three digits in a row.

3. Character Sets and Negation

You can also **negate** a character class by using a caret (^) at the beginning of the square brackets. This negates the match, meaning it will match any character **except** the ones in the set.

For example:

- [^a-z] matches any character **not** a lowercase letter.
- [^0-9] matches any character that is **not** a digit.

This can be helpful when you want to match all characters except a specific set.

4. Real-World Example: Extracting Numeric Data from a Product Description

Suppose we have a product description with varying formats for prices, quantities, and other numeric data, and we need to extract the numeric information. Character classes and ranges can help us achieve this efficiently.

For example, let's say we have the following product description:

bash

```
Product 1: Price - $19.99, Weight - 2.5kg, Stock - 150 units
Product 2: Price - $30.75, Weight - 3.1kg, Stock - 50 units
```

Product 3: Price - $25.50, Weight - 1.8kg, Stock - 220 units

Our goal is to extract all the numeric values (prices, weights, and quantities) from this description. The regex pattern to extract numeric data could be:

python

```
import re

text = """
Product 1: Price - $19.99, Weight - 2.5kg, Stock - 150 units
Product 2: Price - $30.75, Weight - 3.1kg, Stock - 50 units
Product 3: Price - $25.50, Weight - 1.8kg, Stock - 220 units
"""

# Pattern to match prices, weights, and stock numbers
pattern = r'\d+(\.\d+)?'

# Extract numeric values
numbers = re.findall(pattern, text)
print(numbers)
```

Explanation:

- The pattern \d+(\.\d+)? matches:
    - \d+: One or more digits (for whole numbers).
    - (\.\d+)?: An optional decimal part (matches a period followed by one or more digits).

Output:

css

['19.99', '2.5', '150', '30.75', '3.1', '50', '25.50', '1.8', '220']

Here, we successfully extracted all numeric values from the product descriptions, including decimal prices and quantities.

---

5. Practical Tips for Using Character Classes in Python

- **Combining Character Classes**: You can combine character classes to match a variety of characters in different situations. For example, [A-Za-z0-9_] matches alphanumeric characters and underscores (often used for usernames).

- **Use re.findall() to Extract Data**: The re.findall() function returns a list of all matches in a string. It's useful when you want to collect all instances of certain characters (like numeric data) from a large text.

python

```
# Example to extract email addresses
pattern = r'[A-Za-z0-9._%+-]+@[A-Za-z0-9.-]+\.[A-Za-z]{2,}'
emails = re.findall(pattern, "Contact us at support@example.com or admin@mywebsite.org")
print(emails)
```

Output:

css

['support@example.com', 'admin@mywebsite.org']

6.

In this chapter, we've explored **character classes** and **ranges** in regular expressions, which form the foundation of powerful text search and manipulation capabilities. You've learned how to:

- Use shorthand character classes (\d, \w, etc.) for efficient matching.
- Create custom character sets with ranges like [a-z] and [A-Z].
- Apply negation in character sets using [^...].
- Solve a real-world problem by extracting numeric data from a product description using regular expressions.

By mastering these concepts, you'll be well-equipped to handle more complex text manipulation tasks in your Python projects. In the next chapter, we'll dive deeper into more advanced regular expression techniques for matching patterns in text data.

Chapter 6: Special Characters and Escaping

Regular expressions (regex) are a powerful tool for matching and manipulating text. However, to fully leverage regex in Python, it's essential to understand **special characters** and how they function within a regex pattern. These special characters have predefined meanings that can significantly alter the behavior of your pattern. Additionally, certain characters need to be "escaped" so that they are treated as literal characters rather than special symbols.

In this chapter, we will focus on understanding and using special characters in regex, and also discuss how to escape them when necessary. We will then look at a real-world example: **creating a robust regex for HTML tags**, which can be a tricky task due to the varied structures of HTML content.

---

1. Special Characters in Regex

Special characters have specific meanings in regex. They help you build complex search patterns that can match a wide range of strings. Let's break down the most commonly used special characters:

- **. (Dot/Period)**: Matches any single character except newline characters. For example, the pattern a.b will match any string where an a is followed by any character and then followed by b. So it would match acb, a1b, a b, but not ab.

- *** (Asterisk)**: Matches zero or more repetitions of the preceding character or group. For instance, a*b will match b, ab, aab, aaab, and so on. This is useful when you want to match an arbitrary number of a specific character or group of characters.

- **+ (Plus)**: Similar to the asterisk but matches **one or more** occurrences of the preceding element. For example, a+b will match ab, aab, aaab, but not just b (unlike *, which matches b as well).

- **? (Question Mark)**: Makes the preceding character or group optional (zero or one occurrence). For example, a?b will match b and ab, but not aab.

- **{} (Braces)**: Specifies a **specific number** of repetitions. For example, a{3} will match exactly three as (aaa). You can also use ranges like a{2,4}, which will match between 2 and 4 as (aa, aaa, aaaa).

- **[] (Square Brackets)**: Defines a **character class**. It matches any one of the characters enclosed in the brackets. For instance, [abc] will match any of a, b, or c. You can also define ranges like [a-z] to match any lowercase letter or [0-9] to match any digit.

- **() (Parentheses)**: Groups elements together. Parentheses are used to create **capture groups**, which allow you to extract specific portions of the matched text. For example, in the regex (abc)+, the group (abc) is repeated one or more times.

- | **(Pipe)**: This represents a logical **OR**. For example, a|b matches either a or b. You can use this for alternative matches within a pattern.

- \ **(Backslash)**: The backslash is used as an **escape character**. It allows you to use special characters literally or to introduce special sequences like \d for any digit or \w for any alphanumeric character. For example, \. matches a literal dot (.), and \\ matches a literal backslash.

---

2. Escaping Special Characters

In regex, there are times when you want to match characters that are normally considered special. For example, you might want to search for a literal dot (.) rather than any character, or a literal asterisk (*) instead of its meaning as a quantifier.

To match these special characters literally, you need to "escape" them using the backslash (\). The backslash tells the regex engine to treat the following character as literal rather than a special symbol. Here's a list of common characters that might require escaping:

- \.: Matches a literal dot.
- *: Matches a literal asterisk.
- \+: Matches a literal plus sign.

- \?: Matches a literal question mark.
- \{: Matches a literal opening brace.
- \}: Matches a literal closing brace.
- \[and \]: Matches literal square brackets.
- \(and \): Matches literal parentheses.
- \|: Matches a literal pipe.
- \\: Matches a literal backslash.

In practice, escaping is crucial for scenarios where the input data might contain special characters that you want to treat as part of the text.

3. Real-World Example: Creating a Robust Regex for HTML Tags

One of the more challenging tasks when working with text is extracting HTML tags from a webpage or document. HTML tags can have various forms, including attributes, different closing styles, and optional spaces. Let's walk through how to construct a regex to match HTML tags.

Consider the following HTML snippet:

html

```
<div class="content">Welcome to Python Regex!</div>
<a href="https://example.com">Click here</a>
<p>Learn more about regex!</p>
```

To match the HTML tags such as <div>, <a>, and <p>, we could start with a simple regex pattern:

regex

```
<([a-z]+)>
```

- < and > are literal characters for opening and closing the tags.
- [a-z]+ matches one or more lowercase letters (the tag name).

This pattern would match any tag like <div>, <a>, or <p>. However, it doesn't handle attributes or spaces within the tag. To make it more robust, we can improve it as follows:

regex

```
<([a-z]+)(\s+[a-zA-Z0-9\-]+="[^"]*")*\s*>
```

- ([a-z]+): Matches the tag name (e.g., div, a, p).
- (\s+[a-zA-Z0-9\-]+="[^"]*")*: Matches zero or more attributes within the tag. Attributes like class="content" are optional, but if present, they are captured as well.
- \s*: Matches any optional whitespace before the closing >.

This more complex regex will handle simple HTML tags, as well as tags with attributes. While regex is not perfect for parsing HTML in general (due to its complexity), this example shows how powerful regex can be in handling structured text, even with varying formats.

4.

In this chapter, we've covered the most common special characters in regex and learned how to escape them when necessary. You've also seen how these concepts are used in a real-world scenario, such as creating a robust regex for HTML tags.

By mastering the special characters and escaping techniques in regex, you will be able to handle a wide range of text-processing tasks, whether you're cleaning data, validating input, or parsing structured text like HTML. Regular expressions are a versatile tool in Python, and with the knowledge of special characters and how to escape them, you can now build more complex and efficient regex patterns for various applications.

Chapter 7: Quantifiers in Regex

In regular expressions (regex), **quantifiers** define the number of times a particular element (such as a character, word, or group) should be matched in a string. Quantifiers are essential for making your regex patterns more flexible and dynamic. Without quantifiers, your patterns would only match a specific number of characters or repetitions. Quantifiers, however, allow you to tailor your patterns to match a wider variety of text, making them one of the most powerful features in regex.

In this chapter, we will delve into how **quantifiers** work and how they can be combined to create more dynamic and flexible regex patterns. We will also provide real-world examples to illustrate their application, such as matching varying numbers of digits or characters in a string.

---

1. Understanding Quantifiers in Regex

Quantifiers specify how many times a pattern or character should appear. Here are the primary quantifiers used in regex:

- *** (Asterisk)**: Matches zero or more occurrences of the preceding element.

- o Example: a* matches an empty string or any string that contains zero or more a characters (like "", "a", "aa", "aaa").

- **+ (Plus)**: Matches one or more occurrences of the preceding element.

  - o Example: a+ matches strings that contain one or more a characters (like "a", "aa", "aaa"), but not an empty string.

- **? (Question Mark)**: Matches zero or one occurrence of the preceding element. It makes the element optional.

  - o Example: a? matches either an empty string or a string with a single a.

- **{n} (Exact Occurrences)**: Matches exactly n occurrences of the preceding element.

  - o Example: a{3} matches exactly "aaa", but not "aa" or "aaaa".

- **{n,} (At Least n Occurrences)**: Matches n or more occurrences of the preceding element.

  - o Example: a{2,} matches "aa", "aaa", "aaaa", etc.

- **{n,m} (Between n and m Occurrences)**: Matches between n and m occurrences of the preceding element.

  - o Example: a{2,4} matches "aa", "aaa", or "aaaa", but not "a" or "aaaaa".

2. Combining Quantifiers for Flexible Matches

Quantifiers can also be combined to allow for more complex patterns. For instance, if you want to match a string that contains between two and four digits, you could use the pattern \d{2,4}. This pattern would match any string containing two to four digits (e.g., "12", "123", "1234").

Here are a few examples of how quantifiers can be combined:

- **Multiple quantifiers**: \d{2,5}+ — This will match between two and five digits, followed by one or more digits.
- **Quantifiers with other patterns**: \b\w{3,5}\b — This will match words with a length between 3 and 5 characters, using word boundaries (\b).

3. Real-world Example: Matching Varying Numbers of Digits or Characters

One common task in text processing is to match numerical data that may vary in length. For example, phone numbers, ZIP codes, or invoice numbers may have different lengths but follow certain patterns.

Let's consider the task of matching phone numbers in various formats. A common format for phone numbers might look like this:

- (555) 123-4567

- 555-123-4567
- 5551234567
- 123-4567

A regex pattern that can match all these formats might look like:

regex

\(?\d{3}\)?[-\s]?\d{3}[-\s]?\d{4}

Explanation:

- \(? — Matches an optional opening parenthesis (.
- \d{3} — Matches exactly three digits.
- \)? — Matches an optional closing parenthesis).
- [-\s]? — Matches an optional hyphen or space (separating the number groups).
- \d{3} and \d{4} — Match the second and third groups of digits.

This pattern accommodates optional characters like parentheses and hyphens and handles numbers of different lengths.

---

4. Another Example: Matching Product Codes

Suppose you're working with a dataset of products, and each product has a unique product code that follows a specific pattern. The code might look like this:

- ABC-12345

- XYZ-67890
- DEF-54321

A regex to match these product codes could look like:

regex

[A-Z]{3}-\d{5}

Explanation:

- [A-Z]{3} — Matches exactly three uppercase letters.
- - — Matches the hyphen between the letters and the digits.
- \d{5} — Matches exactly five digits.

This pattern ensures that only strings in the format of three letters followed by a hyphen and five digits are matched.

5.

Quantifiers are fundamental to creating flexible and dynamic regex patterns. By understanding and using the key quantifiers (*, +, ?, {n}, {n,}, {n,m}), you can match patterns of varying lengths and complexities. These quantifiers are especially useful when working with real-world data, such as phone numbers, product codes, or ZIP codes, where the number of characters or digits may vary but still follow a predictable pattern.

As we continue with the book, we will dive deeper into combining quantifiers with other regex features to handle more advanced text processing tasks. But for now, the examples above should give you a solid foundation for using quantifiers in your own regex patterns.

Chapter 8: Grouping and Capturing with Parentheses

One of the most powerful and useful features of regular expressions (regex) is the ability to **group** parts of a pattern together. Grouping allows you to combine multiple characters or sub-patterns into one unit, which can then be treated as a single element. This becomes particularly useful when working with complex text patterns or when you need to **capture specific parts** of the match for further processing.

In this chapter, we will explore the concept of **grouping** and **capturing** in regex, focusing on how parentheses () can be used to create groups. We'll also discuss how to **refer to and extract** specific parts of a match for further use. Finally, we'll provide real-world examples of how grouping can be applied to real-world problems, such as extracting the year, month, and day from a date string.

---

1. Using Parentheses for Grouping

In regex, parentheses () are used to group parts of a pattern. This allows you to treat multiple characters or expressions as a single unit. Grouping is important because it helps with **repetition**, **alternation**, and **capturing** specific parts of the match.

Example:

python

import re

text = "The meeting is on 2024-12-16."

```
# Grouping the date part with parentheses
pattern = r"(\d{4})-(\d{2})-(\d{2})"
match = re.search(pattern, text)

if match:
    print(match.group(0))  # Full match: '2024-12-16'
    print(match.group(1))  # Group 1: '2024' (Year)
    print(match.group(2))  # Group 2: '12' (Month)
    print(match.group(3))  # Group 3: '16' (Day)
```

In this example, the pattern (\d{4})-(\d{2})-(\d{2}) groups the date into three parts: the **year**, **month**, and **day**. Each of these parts can be individually referenced using group(1), group(2), and group(3).

---

2. Capturing Groups and Referencing Them

When you use parentheses to group patterns, the content inside those groups is automatically **captured**. This captured content can then be **referenced**, which means you can extract it for further processing or use it in replacements.

In Python, captured groups can be accessed with the .group(n) method, where n is the index of the group you want to extract. The index 0 refers to the full match, while 1, 2, etc., correspond to the individual groups.

Example: Extracting Date Components

python

```
import re

text = "Event scheduled for 2024-12-16 at the main office."

# Pattern to extract the year, month, and day
pattern = r"(\d{4})-(\d{2})-(\d{2})"
match = re.search(pattern, text)

if match:
    # Extract year, month, and day
    year = match.group(1)
    month = match.group(2)
    day = match.group(3)

    print(f"Year: {year}, Month: {month}, Day: {day}")
```

Output:

yaml

```
Year: 2024, Month: 12, Day: 16
```

In this case, the regex captures the components of the date (year, month, and day) separately, which you can then use as needed in the program.

---

3. Nested Grouping

You can also nest groups within other groups, creating a hierarchy of captured elements. This allows you to break down a string into even smaller components.

Example: Extracting Time and Date

python

```
import re

text = "2024-12-16 14:30:00"

# Nested groups for date and time
pattern = r"(\d{4})-(\d{2})-(\d{2}) (\d{2}):(\d{2}):(\d{2})"
match = re.search(pattern, text)

if match:
    date = f"{match.group(1)}-{match.group(2)}-{match.group(3)}"
    time = f"{match.group(4)}:{match.group(5)}:{match.group(6)}"

    print(f"Date: {date}, Time: {time}")
```

Output:

yaml

Date: 2024-12-16, Time: 14:30:00

In this example, we have used **nested groups** to separate both the **date** and **time** components of the string. This makes it easier to process the date and time independently.

---

4. Non-Capturing Groups

Sometimes, you may want to group parts of a pattern for purposes of applying quantifiers or for structuring your pattern without actually capturing the group. For such cases, you can use **non-capturing groups** by adding ?: at the beginning of the group.

Example:

python

```
import re

text = "apple123, banana456, cherry789"

# Non-capturing group to separate the word and number, but don't capture the
word
pattern = r"(\w+)(?:\d+)"
matches = re.findall(pattern, text)

print(matches)  # ['apple', 'banana', 'cherry']
```

In this case, we use a non-capturing group (?:\d+) to group the digits without actually capturing them. The result is that we only capture the words, and the numbers are ignored.

---

5. *Using Capturing Groups in Replacements*

Captured groups can also be used in text replacements. In the re.sub() function, you can refer to captured groups by using \1, \2, etc., in the replacement string.

Example: Swapping Date Format

python

```
import re

text = "2024-12-16"

# Replacing with a new date format
pattern = r"(\d{4})-(\d{2})-(\d{2})"
replacement = r"\3/\2/\1"  # Switch to MM/DD/YYYY format
new_text = re.sub(pattern, replacement, text)

print(new_text)  # Output: 16/12/2024
```

In this example, we capture the year, month, and day, and then use these captured groups to rearrange the date into a new format using \3, \2, and \1.

Real-World Example: Extracting Year, Month, and Day

A real-world use case for grouping and capturing is parsing and extracting date information from strings. Dates can be expressed in many different formats, and regex provides a powerful tool for normalizing these formats or extracting the individual components for further analysis.

Example: Parsing a Log File

python

```python
import re

log = "Error occurred on 2024-12-16 at 14:30:00 in module X"

# Regex to capture date and time
pattern = r"(\d{4})-(\d{2})-(\d{2}) (\d{2}):(\d{2}):(\d{2})"
match = re.search(pattern, log)

if match:
    year, month, day = match.group(1), match.group(2), match.group(3)
    hour, minute, second = match.group(4), match.group(5), match.group(6)

    print(f"Date: {year}-{month}-{day}, Time: {hour}:{minute}:{second}")
```

Output:

yaml

```
Date: 2024-12-16, Time: 14:30:00
```

This example demonstrates how grouping and capturing can be used to parse log entries and extract critical date and time information.

Key Takeaways

- **Parentheses** in regex allow for **grouping** parts of a pattern together, which is essential for complex matches.
- Captured groups are accessed using the .group() method in Python.
- You can use **non-capturing groups** when grouping is needed for structure but you don't want to store the result.
- **Text replacements** using captured groups allow for powerful modifications and transformations in strings.

In the next chapter, we will dive deeper into **lookahead and lookbehind assertions**, which allow you to perform even more powerful regex matching based on what comes before or after a pattern.

Chapter 9: Non-Capturing Groups and Lookahead/Lookbehind Assertions

In the previous chapter, we explored **capturing groups** which allow us to isolate and extract specific parts of a regex match. However, there are situations where you want to **group parts of a pattern** without actually capturing them for later use. This is where **non-capturing groups** and **lookahead/lookbehind assertions** come in. These advanced techniques give you more flexibility in how you match and validate text, without cluttering your matches with unnecessary captures.

This chapter will dive into:

1. **Non-Capturing Groups**: What they are and when to use them.

2. **Lookahead and Lookbehind Assertions**: A way to assert conditions before or after a match, without including them in the match itself.

3. **Real-World Examples**: We will explore how to use these techniques to create more efficient regex patterns, including a real-world example where we validate a password with specific requirements using **lookahead** assertions.

1. Non-Capturing Groups

In regex, a **group** is typically created by enclosing part of a pattern in parentheses (). However, when you don't need to **capture** the matched text for later reference, you can create a **non-capturing group**. This is done by adding ?: at the start of the parentheses.

Syntax:

regex

(?:...)

Example:

regex

(?:abc|def)

This will match either "abc" or "def", but it **won't capture** the matched text for back-referencing. Non-capturing groups are useful when you need to apply quantifiers or alternation (|) within a group but don't need to keep track of the match.

Why Use Non-Capturing Groups?

- **Performance**: Non-capturing groups are faster than capturing groups because the engine doesn't need to store the match.
- **Clarity**: They help keep your regex clean when you don't need the matched portion for later use.

2. Lookahead and Lookbehind Assertions

While regular expressions are primarily used to find patterns, **lookahead** and **lookbehind assertions** give you the ability to match text based on what comes **before** or **after** a pattern, without including it in the match.

Lookahead Assertions

A **lookahead** assertion checks whether a certain pattern **follows** another pattern but does not include it in the match. It's a way to check for conditions without consuming characters from the string.

- **Positive lookahead** ((?=...)): Checks if a certain pattern follows, without including it in the match.
- **Negative lookahead** ((?!...)): Checks that a certain pattern does **not** follow.

Syntax:

- Positive lookahead: a(?=b)
- Negative lookahead: a(?!b)

Example:

regex

\d+(?=\D)

This matches one or more digits (\d+), but only if they are followed by a **non-digit character** (\D). The non-digit character is not included in the match.

Lookbehind Assertions

A **lookbehind** assertion checks whether a certain pattern **precedes** another pattern but does not include it in the match.

- **Positive lookbehind** ((?<=...)): Checks if a certain pattern precedes the current position.
- **Negative lookbehind** ((?<!...)): Checks that a certain pattern does **not** precede the current position.

Syntax:

- Positive lookbehind: (?<=...)
- Negative lookbehind: (?<!)

Example:

regex

(?<=@)\w+

This regex matches a **word** that is **preceded by the "@" symbol** (useful for extracting the domain part of an email).

3. Real-World Example: Validating a Password with Specific Requirements Using Lookahead

Imagine you are tasked with creating a **password validator** that enforces the following rules:

- The password must be at least 8 characters long.
- It must contain at least one uppercase letter.
- It must contain at least one lowercase letter.
- It must contain at least one digit.
- It cannot contain any spaces.

We can use **lookahead assertions** to enforce these rules **without needing to create separate matches for each condition**. Here's how we would approach it with a single regex pattern:

Regex Pattern:

regex

^(?=.*[a-z])(?=.*[A-Z])(?=.*\d)(?!.*\s).{8,}$

Breakdown:

1. ^: Anchors the pattern to the start of the string.
2. (?=.*[a-z]): Positive lookahead to ensure at least one lowercase letter is present.
3. (?=.*[A-Z]): Positive lookahead to ensure at least one uppercase letter is present.

4. (?=.*\d): Positive lookahead to ensure at least one digit is present.

5. (?!.*\s): Negative lookahead to ensure there are no spaces.

6. .{8,}: Ensures that the password is at least 8 characters long.

7. $: Anchors the pattern to the end of the string.

Real-World Use Case:

This pattern can be used in an application that enforces strong password policies. With lookahead assertions, we can validate multiple conditions without needing complex logic, and ensure that all criteria are met before accepting a password.

Key Takeaways

- **Non-capturing groups** allow you to group patterns without storing the matched content, improving performance and clarity.

- **Lookahead** and **lookbehind assertions** provide a way to validate patterns based on what is ahead or behind the current position, without including the matched text in the final match.

- **Real-world examples** of non-capturing groups and assertions include validating passwords and extracting specific parts of strings without unnecessary captures.

MASTERING REGEX WITH PYTHON

In the next chapter, we'll dive deeper into more advanced regex techniques, such as **backreferences** and **conditional expressions**, which will further enhance your ability to process and manipulate text with regex.

Chapter 10: Mastering Anchors and Boundaries

When working with regular expressions, one of the most important concepts to understand is **anchors** and **boundaries**. These elements allow you to control where in a string a match can occur, whether it's at the start, the end, or in the middle. Anchors and boundaries play a crucial role in narrowing down searches to specific patterns and ensuring that your regex is as precise as possible.

In this chapter, we'll dive into the following key topics:

1. **Anchors**: These are special characters that match positions in the string, rather than characters themselves. The two most commonly used anchors are:
    o ^: Matches the start of a string.
    o $: Matches the end of a string.

    Understanding how to use these anchors will allow you to enforce patterns that appear only at the start or end of a string, making your searches more accurate.

2. **Word Boundaries**: Sometimes you only want to match a specific **whole word** rather than partial matches. This is where word boundaries come in:

o \b: Matches a word boundary (between a word character \w and a non-word character).

o \B: Matches a position that is **not** a word boundary.

These boundaries are helpful for making sure that you match **complete words** rather than substrings.

3. **Combining Anchors and Boundaries**: We'll also cover how to combine both anchors and boundaries to create more complex and effective patterns for matching entire sentences, specific words, or sections of a string.

Key Concepts

1. Anchors: ^ and $

Anchors match positions rather than characters, and they allow you to match a pattern only at the start or the end of the string.

- **The caret ^**: This anchor matches the **start** of a string.

  Example:

  o Regex: ^Hello
  o Matches: The word "Hello" only if it appears at the **beginning** of the string. For example, "Hello world!" will match, but "Say Hello" will not.

- **The dollar sign $**: This anchor matches the **end** of a string.

Example:

- o Regex: world!$
- o Matches: The string "world!" only if it appears at the **end** of the string. For example, "Hello world!" will match, but "world! says hello" will not.

2. *Word Boundaries:* \b *and* \B

Word boundaries are useful for matching whole words, ensuring that the pattern is not part of another word.

- **The word boundary \b**: This matches a boundary between a word character (letters, digits, or underscores) and a non-word character (such as spaces or punctuation).

Example:

- o Regex: \bcat\b
- o Matches: The word "cat" as a **whole word**, but will **not** match "catalog" or "scattered" because "cat" is not a whole word in those cases.
- **The non-word boundary \B**: This matches a position that **isn't** a word boundary. It's the opposite of \b, and it's useful when you want to ensure that a pattern **doesn't** occur at a word boundary.

Example:

- o Regex: \Bcat\B
- o Matches: The substring "cat" only when it's **not** surrounded by word boundaries, such as in "scattered catnip", where "cat" is part of another word.

3. Combining Anchors and Boundaries for Advanced Matching

- **Match a full word at the beginning of a sentence**:
  - o Regex: ^The\b
  - o This will match "The" only at the **beginning** of a string, ensuring that the word "The" is not part of another word.
- **Match a full sentence**:
  - o Regex: ^\bThis\b.*\btext\b$
  - o This matches the **exact** sentence that starts with "This" and ends with "text".

Real-World Example: Validating Whole Words and Sentences

Let's consider a scenario where you're working with user input in a search function. You need to ensure that the user query matches **whole words** rather than partial words. Here's how you can use anchors and boundaries:

Problem: Validate whether a search term exactly matches the words "apple" or "orange" (i.e., "apple" should not be part of a longer word like "applesauce").

Solution: You can use the word boundary anchor \b to ensure you're matching only full words:

- Regex: \b(apple|orange)\b
- This will match "apple" or "orange" **only if they are standalone words**.

If the user enters "I like applesauce," the regex will **not match** because "apple" is part of the word "applesauce."

In this chapter, we've learned how **anchors** and **boundaries** can be used to refine regex patterns for better accuracy and control over text matching. These powerful tools allow us to match specific positions in a string, whether it's the start, end, or a boundary between words. By mastering anchors and boundaries, you'll be able to craft highly targeted regex patterns for tasks like word validation, text parsing, and more complex pattern matching in various real-world scenarios.

Chapter 11: Backreferences and Recursion

In the world of regular expressions, **backreferences** and **recursion** are powerful, yet sometimes underutilized, tools that can help solve complex string-matching problems. They allow you to reference previous parts of your regex pattern and even define patterns that can repeat themselves, which is especially useful for matching nested structures like parentheses, HTML tags, or other recursive patterns.

In this chapter, we'll explore two advanced techniques in regular expressions: **backreferences** and **recursion**. We'll break them down with examples and show you how to apply them to solve real-world problems.

1. Backreferences in Regex

A **backreference** allows you to match the same text that was matched by a previous part of the regular expression. This is useful when you need to ensure that a certain part of the string repeats in the same way it appeared earlier.

Syntax:

- In Python's re module, backreferences are referenced using \N, where N is the number of the capturing group. For example:
  - (\d+)\s+\1 will match any number followed by spaces and the same number again.

Example:

Let's say you want to match pairs of identical words in a string, like "hello hello" or "test test". You can do this with a backreference.

python

```
import re

text = "hello hello world world test test"
pattern = r"(\b\w+\b) \1"  # \1 refers to the first capturing group

matches = re.findall(pattern, text)
print(matches)
```

Explanation:

- (\b\w+\b) captures a word (using word boundaries to ensure we're matching entire words).
- \1 refers back to the first capturing group, ensuring that the word matches exactly again.

Output:

python

['hello', 'world', 'test']

In this case, the pattern finds all pairs of identical words in the string.

2. Recursion in Regex

Recursion in regular expressions allows a pattern to call itself, which is particularly useful for matching nested structures such as parentheses, HTML tags, or mathematical expressions. Recursive regex patterns enable you to handle cases where the structure you're trying to match is inherently recursive or self-referential.

While not all regular expression engines support recursion, Python's re module doesn't support this feature natively, but we can demonstrate how recursion can be used in regex engines that do, such as PCRE (Perl Compatible Regular Expressions), which are supported in tools like regex (a third-party Python library).

Example: Matching Nested Parentheses

Let's consider an example where we need to match a string containing nested parentheses. While simple regex patterns can match basic parentheses, handling nested parentheses requires a recursive approach.

A recursive pattern might look like this in PCRE-compatible regex engines:

regex

\(((?:[^()]+|(?R))*\)

- \(and \) match literal parentheses.
- (?:[^()]+|(?R))* matches content inside the parentheses, either non-parenthesis characters or recursively matching the entire pattern again.

Explanation of Recursion:

- (?R) is a recursive call, meaning the pattern will continue to apply itself whenever a nested set of parentheses is found. This ensures that the regex can match nested parentheses at any level.

Although recursion is not directly supported by Python's re module, the regex package (an enhanced version of Python's re module) allows for recursive patterns. Here's how you can implement the above example using the regex module:

python

```
import regex as re

text = "(a(b(c)d)e)f"
pattern = r"\(((?:[^()]+|(?R))*\)"

matches = re.findall(pattern, text)
print(matches)
```

Output:

python

['(a(b(c)d)e)', '(b(c)d)', '(c)']

This example matches all levels of nested parentheses, demonstrating how recursion in regular expressions can handle complex, nested data structures.

3. Real-World Example: Matching Nested HTML Tags

Another common use case for backreferences and recursion is parsing HTML-like structures. Consider an example where you need to extract matching opening and closing HTML tags, such as <div>...</div> or <a>...</a>. To handle this, you'll need both backreferences (to ensure matching tags) and recursion (to deal with nested tags).

In a simplified example using recursion (again, this works in engines that support it like PCRE):

regex

<(\w+)>(?:[^<]+|(?R))*</\1>

- <(\w+)> matches an opening tag and captures the tag name.
- (?:[^<]+|(?R))* matches content inside the tag, which could be anything except another tag or recursively matched nested tags.

- <∧1> ensures that the tag closes with the same tag name captured in the first group.

This pattern matches HTML-like tags with potentially nested content.

4. Practical Considerations for Using Backreferences and Recursion

While backreferences and recursion are powerful, they are also more computationally expensive than basic regex patterns. Here are a few things to consider:

- **Performance**: Recursive patterns can cause performance issues, especially when matching deeply nested structures. It's important to balance readability and efficiency.
- **Use Cases**: Backreferences are very useful for finding repeated data, while recursion is ideal for parsing nested or hierarchical data structures.
- **Alternatives**: In cases where regex becomes too complex, consider using specialized parsers (like HTML parsers or CSV readers) to handle the data more efficiently and accurately.

:

In this chapter, we've covered two advanced features of regular expressions: **backreferences** and **recursion**. Backreferences allow you to reference parts of the pattern that were matched earlier, making it possible to match repeated data, such as duplicated words or characters. Recursion enables you to handle complex and nested structures, such as parentheses or HTML tags, in your text data. Both techniques are incredibly powerful but should be used carefully due to their complexity and potential performance costs.

In the next chapter, we'll look into even more advanced techniques, like advanced lookahead/lookbehind assertions, that can make your regex skills even more powerful.

Chapter 12: Regex Performance and Optimization

Regular expressions (regex) are incredibly powerful tools for text processing, but as patterns become more complex and data sets grow larger, performance can become a concern. In this chapter, we will dive into the factors that influence the performance of regex operations and explore how you can optimize your patterns to achieve faster, more efficient results.

1. Understanding Regex Performance

Regex performance is primarily determined by how well the pattern is constructed and how it interacts with the input data. While regex is generally fast for small-scale tasks, certain patterns, especially complex ones, can lead to **performance bottlenecks**.

Factors that impact regex performance:

- **Backtracking:** Regex engines often use a technique called backtracking to try different possibilities when attempting to match a pattern. While backtracking is necessary in many cases, it can result in **exponential time complexity** if the regex is poorly designed, especially with patterns that contain nested quantifiers (e.g., .* or .*?) or groups.

- **Greedy vs. Lazy Matching:** Greedy quantifiers (e.g., *, +) try to match as much text as possible, which can lead to unnecessary backtracking. Lazy quantifiers (e.g., *?, +?) match the smallest possible text, which can speed up matching in some cases.

- **Complexity of the Pattern:** More complex regex patterns require more computation. Patterns with many groups, nested quantifiers, and lookaheads/lookbehinds can lead to slower performance.

2. Identifying Performance Bottlenecks

In Python, the re library uses **backtracking** to attempt all possible matches of a given pattern. If you have a regex that is unnecessarily complex or poorly optimized, it can result in significant delays, especially when applied to large datasets.

A few examples of patterns that could lead to performance problems:

- **Nested Quantifiers:** Patterns like (.*)+ or (a+)+ can cause excessive backtracking. The regex engine tries all possible combinations of matches, which may result in very slow performance for larger inputs.

- **Overuse of Lookaheads and Lookbehinds:** Lookaheads and lookbehinds are powerful but computationally expensive features. Using them in complex patterns may reduce the overall performance of your regex.

- **Matching Long Strings with Greedy Quantifiers:** If you're trying to match a large portion of a string with a greedy quantifier like .*, the regex engine will scan through the entire string, leading to high processing costs.

3. Optimizing Regex for Speed

Once you've identified the performance bottlenecks, you can apply various optimization strategies to improve regex performance. Here are some techniques:

a. Use Atomic Groups and Non-Greedy Quantifiers

Atomic groups (?>...) allow the regex engine to avoid backtracking within that part of the pattern. If you have a section of the pattern that can be matched without backtracking, using atomic groups can improve performance.

Similarly, using non-greedy quantifiers (*?, +?) will limit the number of attempts the engine has to make.

python

```
# Example of a greedy vs non-greedy pattern
text = "The quick brown fox jumps over the lazy dog"

# Greedy match (slower for large text)
greedy_pattern = r"quick.*dog"

# Non-greedy match (faster in many cases)
```

```
non_greedy_pattern = r"quick.*?dog"
```

b. Pre-compile Regex Patterns

In Python, you can use the re.compile() function to pre-compile a regex pattern before using it multiple times. This reduces the overhead of compiling the pattern each time.

python

```
import re

# Pre-compiling the regex pattern
pattern = re.compile(r"\b(\w+)\b")

# Using pre-compiled pattern
matches = pattern.findall("This is a simple sentence.")
```

c. Use re.search() Over re.findall() When Applicable

re.search() stops as soon as it finds a match, whereas re.findall() will attempt to find **all** matches in the input string, which may not always be necessary. If you're only interested in the first match, re.search() will be faster.

python

```
import re

# Faster approach if you're looking for just the first match
match = re.search(r"\d+", "There are 123 numbers here.")
```

d. Avoid Backreferences in Complex Patterns

Backreferences can be useful but can also slow down performance if used excessively in large or complex patterns. If possible, try to avoid them or limit their use to simpler scenarios.

e. Optimize Your Regular Expression Syntax

In many cases, a seemingly complex regex pattern can be simplified. For instance, matching words or numbers using \w+ can be more efficient than using [a-zA-Z0-9]+ or [0-9]+ for digits. Simplify your patterns wherever possible.

4. Real-World Example: Performance Considerations in Log File Parsing

Let's walk through a real-world example where performance is key: **log file parsing**. Log files can grow very large, and inefficient regex patterns could slow down the process.

Scenario: We want to extract error messages from a log file that contains thousands of lines. A regex pattern like ".*Error.*" is quite inefficient because it is greedy and will scan through the entire line for every match, which is very slow on large files.

Inefficient approach:

python

import re

```
log_data = """
INFO: Starting process
ERROR: Failed to load module
INFO: Process complete
ERROR: Connection timeout
"""


# Greedy match (slow on large data)
error_pattern = r".*Error.*"


matches = re.findall(error_pattern, log_data)
```

Optimized approach:

To optimize this, we can use a non-greedy pattern that matches only the relevant part of the line, and we can compile the regex to avoid recompiling it multiple times.

python

```
import re


log_data = """
INFO: Starting process
ERROR: Failed to load module
INFO: Process complete
ERROR: Connection timeout
"""


# Pre-compile the regex pattern and use non-greedy matching
error_pattern = re.compile(r"^Error.*?$")
```

```
matches = error_pattern.findall(log_data)
```

By pre-compiling the pattern and simplifying the matching process, we can make the code much faster, especially as the size of the log file grows.

5. Profiling Regex Performance

To further optimize your regex, it's important to profile the performance of different patterns. In Python, you can use the timeit module to measure how long your regex patterns take to execute.

python

```
import timeit

# Time the execution of a regex pattern
execution_time = timeit.timeit(lambda: re.findall(r".*Error.*", log_data), number=1000)
print(f"Execution time: {execution_time} seconds")
```

This allows you to compare the performance of different regex patterns and choose the one that best balances efficiency and readability.

6. Best Practices for Regex Performance

- **Keep regex patterns simple:** Avoid using unnecessary groups, quantifiers, or lookaheads when simpler alternatives exist.

- **Profile your code:** Measure performance using profiling tools like timeit to ensure that regex is not the bottleneck.

- **Use specific character classes:** Instead of using .*, use specific character classes (e.g., \d+, \w+) for more targeted matching.

- **Pre-compile patterns for repeated use:** Compile your regex patterns with re.compile() when they are used multiple times.

Regex can be incredibly fast and efficient, but its performance largely depends on how you structure your patterns and how you apply them to your data. By understanding the factors that influence regex performance and applying best practices for optimization, you can ensure that your regex solutions remain scalable, even when working with large datasets or complex patterns.

In this chapter, we have covered the key performance considerations when using regular expressions in Python and provided real-world examples to demonstrate how to optimize regex for speed. By incorporating these tips and techniques, you'll be able to handle even the most challenging text processing tasks with greater efficiency.

Chapter 13: Regex Flags in Python

Regex flags are special options that you can use to modify the behavior of a regular expression. These flags allow you to control various aspects of matching, such as case sensitivity, multi-line matching, and dot behavior. In Python, flags are passed as arguments to the functions in the re module (such as re.match(), re.search(), re.findall(), and re.sub()), providing a flexible way to adjust how regex patterns interact with the input data.

In this chapter, we'll explore some of the most commonly used regex flags in Python, how to implement them, and real-world examples of their usage.

1. Understanding Regex Flags

Regex flags are set of parameters that control how the regex engine interprets your regular expression pattern. In Python, flags are typically passed as arguments in the functions of the re module. Here's a breakdown of the most commonly used flags:

- **re.I (re.IGNORECASE):** This flag allows case-insensitive matching, meaning it will match both uppercase and lowercase letters.

- **re.M (re.MULTILINE):** With this flag, the behavior of the ^ (start of string) and $ (end of string) anchors changes. In multi-line strings, ^ matches the beginning of a line, and $

matches the end of a line, not just the beginning and end of the entire string.

- **re.S (re.DOTALL):** This flag allows the dot (.) character to match newlines (\n). Normally, the dot does not match line breaks, but with re.S, it matches any character, including line breaks.

- **re.X (re.VERBOSE):** This flag allows you to write more readable and understandable regular expressions. It lets you add whitespace and comments inside the regex pattern without affecting its functionality, making your regex patterns cleaner.

2. How to Use Flags to Modify Matching Behavior

To use flags in Python, simply pass them as an additional argument to the regex function. You can use one or more flags at a time. The syntax looks like this:

python

```
import re

pattern = r"some pattern"

# Using a single flag
re.match(pattern, string, flags=re.I)

# Using multiple flags
```

re.findall(pattern, string, flags=re.M | re.S)

3. Real-World Example: Case-Insensitive Matching for URLs

One of the most common use cases for the re.I flag is matching text where case sensitivity should be ignored. For example, let's say you want to extract URLs from a document, but URLs might be written in different cases (e.g., HTTP://, https://, Http://). Using the re.I flag ensures that all URLs, regardless of case, are matched.

Code Example:

python

```
import re

# Sample text with different cases for URLs
text = """
Visit our site at HTTP://example.com for more info.
Alternatively, you can use https://www.example.com.
"""

# Regex pattern to match URLs (case-insensitive)
pattern = r"https?://\S+"  # Matches 'http' or 'https' followed by '://', and non-whitespace characters

# Use the re.I flag to make the match case-insensitive
urls = re.findall(pattern, text, flags=re.I)
```

```
# Print the matched URLs
print(urls)
```

Output:

css

['HTTP://example.com', 'https://www.example.com']

Explanation:

- The regex pattern r"https?://\S+" matches URLs that start with http or https followed by :// and any non-whitespace characters.
- By passing flags=re.I, the regex engine ignores case, ensuring it matches both HTTP:// and https:// regardless of their case.

4. Combining Flags for Advanced Matching

Often, you'll need to use more than one flag to handle complex matching scenarios. For example, when processing multi-line data where you want to match the start or end of each line (not just the beginning or end of the entire string), you can combine the re.M flag with others like re.I for case-insensitive matching.

Code Example: Multi-Line and Case-Insensitive Matching
python

import re

Sample text with multiple lines

```
text = """
John: 25
john: 30
Jane: 22
"""
```

```
# Regex pattern to match names followed by ages (case-insensitive)
pattern = r"^([a-zA-Z]+): (\d+)$"
```

```
# Use both re.M (multi-line matching) and re.I (case-insensitive matching)
matches = re.findall(pattern, text, flags=re.M | re.I)
```

```
# Print the matched names and ages
print(matches)
```

Output:

css

```
[('John', '25'), ('john', '30'), ('Jane', '22')]
```

Explanation:

- The pattern r"^([a-zA-Z]+): (\d+)$" matches a name followed by a colon and age on each line.
- The re.M flag ensures that ^ and $ match the beginning and end of each line, not just the start and end of the entire string.
- The re.I flag allows the pattern to match names regardless of whether they are written as John, john, or JANE.

5. Practical Use Cases for Regex Flags

- **re.I (re.IGNORECASE):** Useful for matching case-insensitive data like URLs, email addresses, or usernames.

- **re.M (re.MULTILINE):** Essential when working with multi-line strings such as logs, configuration files, or text files.

- **re.S (re.DOTALL):** Helpful when you need to match across multiple lines, such as in processing HTML content or extracting information from large text blobs.

- **re.X (re.VERBOSE):** Great for writing complex regex patterns, as it allows you to add comments and format the regex for readability, especially when dealing with long, intricate patterns.

6.

Regex flags provide a powerful mechanism for modifying the behavior of your regular expressions, enabling you to create more flexible and efficient search patterns. By understanding and applying these flags appropriately, you can fine-tune your regex to handle diverse use cases, such as case-insensitive matching, multi-line processing, and more. In real-world scenarios, leveraging these flags helps streamline text processing tasks, whether you're extracting data from log files, validating user input, or performing advanced search operations across large datasets.

Chapter 14: Text Search and Extraction

Regular expressions (regex) are an essential tool for searching, extracting, and manipulating text in Python. When working with large datasets, especially in text-heavy formats like CSV files, logs, or HTML, regex can save you a significant amount of time by automating the process of searching and extracting specific patterns.

In this chapter, we will delve into the practical aspects of using regex to search through large text files and extract relevant data. We will also cover the performance considerations and best practices for text extraction using Python's re library.

1. Searching and Extracting Data with Regex

Searching for specific patterns within large datasets often requires precise matching. Regex allows you to define complex search criteria, from simple word matches to more intricate patterns like dates, emails, or URLs. By using regex, we can filter out the necessary pieces of data from unstructured text files, making it easier to analyze.

Key Steps in Regex Search and Extraction:

1. **Defining the Pattern**: First, you need to identify the specific pattern you're looking for within your text. This can range

from extracting email addresses, phone numbers, product codes, or financial amounts.

2. **Applying the Regex Function**: Using functions like re.findall() or re.search(), you can apply the defined regex pattern to your data. findall() returns all non-overlapping matches, while search() returns only the first match.

3. **Post-processing**: After extracting the data, you may need to clean or format it before using it in further analysis, especially when dealing with data inconsistencies.

---

2. Real-World Example: Extracting Data from a CSV File Using Regex

Let's look at an example where we need to extract specific data from a CSV file using regex. Imagine you have a CSV file containing information about a set of products, and you want to extract all the product IDs, prices, and categories.

Sample Data (products.csv):

csv

```
product_id,product_name,price,category
P12345,Widget A,19.99,Electronics
P67890,Widget B,29.99,Home
P11223,Widget C,14.99,Electronics
P33445,Widget D,9.99,Kitchen
```

Objective:

We want to extract the product IDs (which follow the format PXXXXX), the price (which is a float), and the category (which is a word).

Steps for Extraction:

1. **Define the Regex Pattern**:
   - The product ID: This will follow the pattern P followed by five digits. So, the pattern will be: r'P\d{5}'.
   - The price: We are looking for a float value, so we can use the pattern: r'\d+\.\d{2}'.
   - The category: Since it's a single word, the regex pattern would be: r'[A-Za-z]+'.

2. **Writing the Code**:

python

```
import re
import csv

# Open the CSV file
with open('products.csv', 'r') as file:
    reader = csv.reader(file)
    headers = next(reader)  # Skip the header row

    # Define regex patterns for product ID, price, and category
```

```
product_id_pattern = r'P\d{5}'
price_pattern = r'\d+\.\d{2}'
category_pattern = r'[A-Za-z]+'


# Iterate through each row and extract data using regex
for row in reader:
    product_id = re.search(product_id_pattern, row[0]).group()   # Extract product_id from first column
    price = re.search(price_pattern, row[2]).group()  # Extract price from third column
    category = re.search(category_pattern, row[3]).group()  # Extract category from fourth column


    # Print extracted information
    print(f"Product ID: {product_id}, Price: {price}, Category: {category}")
```

Output:
yaml

Product ID: P12345, Price: 19.99, Category: Electronics

Product ID: P67890, Price: 29.99, Category: Home

Product ID: P11223, Price: 14.99, Category: Electronics

Product ID: P33445, Price: 9.99, Category: Kitchen

---

3. Performance Considerations

When working with large text files or data stored in CSV, XML, or JSON formats, regex search operations can become computationally expensive, especially if the text is unstructured or if you're applying complex patterns. Here are some performance considerations:

- **Efficiency of Patterns**: Simple patterns like matching digits (\d) or letters ([A-Za-z]) are faster than more complex patterns like nested groups or backreferences.
- **Using findall() vs search()**: findall() will return all matches, whereas search() stops after the first match is found. If you only need the first match, search() will be more efficient.
- **Avoiding Redundant Matching**: Avoid running the same regex pattern multiple times on the same text. Instead, try to extract all necessary information in one go.

4. Best Practices for Efficient Text Extraction

- **Use Raw Strings**: In Python, always use raw strings (prefix the string with r) when writing regex patterns to avoid issues with escape characters.
- **Precompile Regex Patterns**: If you're using the same regex pattern multiple times, compile the pattern using re.compile() to improve performance, as the regex engine will not need to recompile the pattern each time.

python

```
compiled_pattern = re.compile(r'P\d{5}')
product_id = compiled_pattern.search(row[0]).group()
```

- **Handle Exceptions**: Always handle cases where a regex match may fail. Using try-except blocks around group() calls will prevent errors when a match isn't found.

5.

In this chapter, we covered how to use regex in Python to search and extract data from large text files, with a practical example of extracting information from a CSV file. Regex is an invaluable tool for processing and extracting data from unstructured text, and when combined with Python, it enables you to efficiently handle and manipulate large datasets. By mastering these techniques, you can streamline your data cleaning, transformation, and analysis processes.

In the next chapter, we will explore advanced text manipulation techniques, including substitutions and replacements using regex in Python.

Chapter 15: Data Cleaning with Regex

Data cleaning is a critical step in any data analysis or machine learning project. Data often comes in messy, unstructured formats, making it challenging to process. Regular expressions (regex) offer a powerful and flexible way to clean and preprocess this data by identifying patterns, removing unwanted characters, and filling in gaps.

In this chapter, we will explore how to leverage Python's re library for cleaning and preprocessing text data. By the end of this chapter, you'll be equipped with the knowledge to use regex for tasks like handling missing values, fixing malformed data, and transforming text into a clean, structured format for analysis.

---

1. Using Regex to Clean and Preprocess Messy Data

Messy data can include everything from extra spaces, special characters, and unwanted symbols, to inconsistent formats. Regex helps automate the identification and removal of these anomalies in a way that is both efficient and scalable.

Common data cleaning tasks that can be handled with regex include:

- **Trimming unnecessary white spaces.**
- **Removing unwanted characters.**

- **Standardizing data formats (e.g., phone numbers, dates).**
- **Splitting and restructuring data.**

Example: Cleaning Whitespace and Punctuation

Imagine you have a dataset with inconsistent white spaces and unnecessary punctuation around financial numbers. You can use regex to clean up this data:

python

```
import re

# Sample text with excess whitespace and unwanted punctuation
text = "Total amount:   $1,200 , Balance: $  3,456 ."

# Remove extra spaces and punctuation around financial numbers
cleaned_text = re.sub(r'\s+', ' ', text)  # Replace multiple spaces with a single space
cleaned_text = re.sub(r'[^\w\s.,]', '', cleaned_text)   # Remove any non-alphanumeric characters except . and ,
print(cleaned_text)
```

Output:

bash

```
Total amount: $1,200 , Balance: $3,456 .
```

---

2. Handling Missing or Malformed Data Using Regex

Missing or malformed data is another common challenge in data cleaning. In many cases, data can be incomplete or contain placeholders (like "N/A" or "null") that need to be handled before analysis. Regex can be used to detect these patterns and replace them with appropriate values.

Example: Replacing Missing Values

Let's say a dataset includes entries for missing financial values marked by "N/A". You can replace these with None or any other placeholder that fits the context.

python

```python
# Sample dataset with "N/A" as a placeholder for missing values
data = ["$1,200", "N/A", "$3,456", "N/A", "$5,000"]

# Replace "N/A" with None
cleaned_data = [None if re.match(r'N/A', value) else value for value in data]
print(cleaned_data)
```

Output:

python

```python
['$1,200', None, '$3,456', None, '$5,000']
```

This allows you to effectively manage missing data points in your dataset, ensuring they don't cause errors during analysis or processing.

3. Real-World Example: Cleaning Financial Data from Text Files

Financial datasets often come in the form of unstructured text files. These may contain tables, unformatted numerical data, or even mixed text with numeric values. Let's consider a financial report with various data points that need cleaning:

Example: Financial Data Cleaning from a Text File

python

```
import re

# Simulated financial data in text format
raw_data = """
Report for 2022:
Total Revenue: $2,100,000
Net Income :   $ 300,000
Operating Expenses: $450,000
Gross Margin: $1,750,000
"""


# Regex pattern to clean financial values and remove excess spaces
cleaned_data = re.sub(r'\s+', ' ', raw_data)  # Remove excess spaces
cleaned_data = re.sub(r'\s*([:,$])\s*', r'\1', cleaned_data)  # Remove spaces around symbols
cleaned_data = re.sub(r'\$', '', cleaned_data)  # Remove currency symbol for analysis
print(cleaned_data)
```

Output:

mathematica

Report for 2022: Total Revenue: 2100000 Net Income: 300000 Operating Expenses: 450000 Gross Margin: 1750000

In this example:

- **Excess spaces** between words and symbols were replaced with single spaces.
- **Currency symbols** were removed to focus on the numeric values.

The cleaned data is now more structured and ready for further analysis.

---

4. Using Regex to Format and Standardize Data

Regex can also help you format and standardize inconsistent data formats. For example, phone numbers, social security numbers, and financial figures often come in various formats that need to be standardized.

Example: Formatting Phone Numbers

python

```
# Sample phone numbers with different formats
```

```
phone_numbers = ["123-456-7890", "(123) 456-7890", "123.456.7890"]

# Standardizing to the format (XXX) XXX-XXXX
formatted_numbers = [re.sub(r'(\d{3})[-.\s]?\(?(?(\d{3})\))?[-.\s]?(\d{4})', r'(\1) \2-\3', number) for number in phone_numbers]
print(formatted_numbers)
```

Output:

css

```
['(123) 456-7890', '(123) 456-7890', '(123) 456-7890']
```

This example demonstrates how regex can help standardize phone numbers by ensuring they all conform to the same format.

---

5. Best Practices for Using Regex in Data Cleaning

While regex is incredibly powerful, it's important to follow best practices to ensure efficiency and readability:

- **Keep patterns simple**: Regex patterns can get complex very quickly. Keep them as simple as possible to improve readability and maintainability.

- **Use non-greedy matching when needed**: Greedy matches can cause unwanted results, especially when working with multiline strings. Use ? to make patterns non-greedy.

- **Test your patterns**: Regex can be tricky. Always test your patterns against sample data before applying them to your entire dataset.

6.

Regex is an indispensable tool for cleaning and preprocessing messy data. With Python's re library, you can automate tasks like removing unwanted characters, fixing malformed entries, handling missing data, and transforming data into the right format. Whether you are cleaning financial data, text documents, or any other type of unstructured data, regex provides the flexibility and power to tackle complex cleaning tasks efficiently.

In this chapter, we've seen practical examples of how regex can streamline the data cleaning process. As you continue to explore regex and Python, you'll uncover even more powerful ways to process and clean your data for deeper insights and analysis.

This chapter has provided a solid foundation for understanding how to use regex for data cleaning. In the next chapter, we will explore more advanced applications of regex in real-world scenarios, including how to integrate regex with other Python tools and libraries for enhanced data processing workflows.

Chapter 16: Web Scraping with Regex

Web scraping is an essential skill for collecting data from the internet. Whether you need to extract product prices, articles, or any other type of data, web scraping allows you to gather that information automatically, saving time and resources. Regular expressions (regex) can be a powerful tool when combined with Python libraries like requests and BeautifulSoup to efficiently parse and extract relevant content from web pages.

In this chapter, we will cover how to use regex for web scraping tasks, how to combine it with the requests library to retrieve web content, and how to use BeautifulSoup to navigate HTML documents. We will also demonstrate a practical, real-world example of scraping product data from an e-commerce website, such as product names, prices, and descriptions.

1. Extracting Data from Web Pages Using Regex

When scraping websites, the goal is often to extract specific pieces of information embedded in HTML. Regex allows us to target exact patterns and retrieve relevant text quickly and efficiently.

Here are some key steps to consider when using regex for web scraping:

- **Fetching the Web Page**: First, you'll need to fetch the HTML content of the page using a library like requests.

- **Writing Regex Patterns**: Once the HTML content is retrieved, you can write regex patterns to find specific tags, classes, or identifiers where the data resides.

- **Extracting Data**: You can use regex to match and extract specific portions of text, such as product names, prices, and descriptions, by finding the corresponding HTML elements and their contents.

Example:

python

```
import requests
import re

# Fetching the page content
url = 'https://example.com/products'
response = requests.get(url)
html_content = response.text

# Regex pattern to match product names
pattern = r'<h2 class="product-name">([^<]+)</h2>'
product_names = re.findall(pattern, html_content)

print(product_names)
```

In the above example, the regex pattern matches any text enclosed within <h2 class="product-name"> and </h2>. The re.findall() method is used to return all occurrences of the pattern (i.e., all product names) in the HTML content.

2. Combining Regex with Python Libraries like Requests and BeautifulSoup

While regex can be incredibly powerful for extracting simple patterns from HTML, libraries like BeautifulSoup offer a more structured approach to parsing and navigating HTML documents. However, regex can still be used effectively in combination with BeautifulSoup for specific tasks, such as extracting data from text content once the HTML elements have been identified.

Steps to combine regex with BeautifulSoup:

- **Fetch the web page**: Use requests to retrieve the HTML of the page.
- **Parse HTML with BeautifulSoup**: Use BeautifulSoup to navigate the HTML tree structure.
- **Use regex within BeautifulSoup**: Apply regex on extracted text content to filter or clean up data further.

Example:

python

```
from bs4 import BeautifulSoup
import requests
```

```
import re

# Fetch the page content
url = 'https://example.com/products'
response = requests.get(url)
soup = BeautifulSoup(response.text, 'html.parser')

# Extract all product descriptions using BeautifulSoup
product_descriptions = soup.find_all('div', class_='product-description')

# Use regex to clean the descriptions
cleaned_descriptions = [re.sub(r'\s+', ' ', description.text.strip()) for description in product_descriptions]

print(cleaned_descriptions)
```

In this example:

- BeautifulSoup is used to parse the HTML and extract all product descriptions from the div tags with the class product-description.

- Regex (re.sub) is then applied to clean the text by removing extra whitespace and formatting it.

3. Real-World Example: Scraping Product Information from an E-commerce Website

Let's walk through a more comprehensive example of scraping product information from an e-commerce website. We'll extract the product name, price, and description and then clean the data using regex.

Step-by-Step Example:

python

```
import requests
from bs4 import BeautifulSoup
import re

# Step 1: Fetch the webpage content
url = 'https://example-ecommerce.com/products'
response = requests.get(url)
soup = BeautifulSoup(response.text, 'html.parser')

# Step 2: Extract product names
product_names = [name.text for name in soup.find_all('h2', class_='product-name')]

# Step 3: Extract product prices (prices often contain symbols and commas, so use regex to clean)
price_pattern = r'\$([\d,]+(?:\.\d{2})?)'
product_prices = [re.search(price_pattern, price.text).group(1) if re.search(price_pattern, price.text) else 'N/A'
        for price in soup.find_all('span', class_='product-price')]

# Step 4: Extract product descriptions
product_descriptions = [desc.text.strip() for desc in soup.find_all('p', class_='product-description')]
```

```
# Step 5: Clean up the extracted data using regex
cleaned_product_names = [re.sub(r'\s+', ' ', name.strip()) for name in
product_names]
cleaned_descriptions = [re.sub(r'\s+', ' ', desc.strip()) for desc in
product_descriptions]

# Step 6: Display results
for i in range(len(cleaned_product_names)):
    print(f"Product Name: {cleaned_product_names[i]}")
    print(f"Price: ${product_prices[i]}")
    print(f"Description: {cleaned_descriptions[i]}")
    print('-' * 50)
```

In this example, we:

1. Use requests to fetch the HTML content from the e-commerce site.

2. Use BeautifulSoup to parse the content and extract product names, prices, and descriptions.

3. Apply regex to clean the price values, extracting just the numeric value and ensuring it is in the proper format.

4. Clean the product names and descriptions using regex to remove any extra spaces or formatting inconsistencies.

4. Best Practices and Considerations for Web Scraping with Regex

While regex is powerful, it's important to consider a few best practices:

- **Respect Website Terms of Service**: Always check a website's robots.txt file to understand the scraping rules and adhere to them.

- **Handle Errors Gracefully**: Be sure to handle edge cases, such as missing data or malformed HTML, with appropriate error handling.

- **Optimize Performance**: Scraping large websites can lead to performance issues. Use techniques like limiting requests, handling timeouts, and avoiding unnecessary regex operations to optimize speed.

5.

Web scraping with regex is a crucial skill for extracting structured data from the unstructured web. When combined with Python libraries like requests and BeautifulSoup, regex allows you to efficiently navigate and extract data from complex HTML structures. By following the examples and best practices in this chapter, you can start building your own web scraping tools to gather valuable data from the web.

Chapter 17: Log File Parsing and Analysis with Regex

Log files are essential for tracking and monitoring various activities in systems, servers, applications, and websites. Whether it's for debugging, performance monitoring, or security analysis, log files provide a wealth of information that can be invaluable. However, extracting meaningful data from log files can be a challenge, especially when dealing with large volumes of data or complex log formats. This is where regular expressions (regex) come in handy.

Regex is a powerful tool for parsing and analyzing log files because it allows you to search for specific patterns, extract data, and automate the analysis process. In this chapter, we will explore how to use regex to parse different types of log files, identify common patterns, and extract valuable insights. We will also look at how regex can help in error tracking, performance monitoring, and security auditing.

---

1. Understanding Log Files

Before diving into regex, it's important to understand the structure of typical log files. Log files generally consist of time-stamped records that capture a variety of events, including user actions, system operations, errors, and warnings.

Common log file types include:

- **Web server logs**: Record HTTP requests, client IPs, user agents, etc.
- **System logs**: Track system processes, services, and errors.
- **Application logs**: Contain application-specific messages like errors, exceptions, and information.
- **Security logs**: Capture security-related events such as authentication attempts, access violations, and malware detections.

While each log type may have its own structure, they generally follow a predictable pattern that can be captured with regex.

---

2. Common Log File Patterns

Log files often include repeated patterns that are used to represent various data points such as timestamps, IP addresses, URLs, error codes, and more. Below are some examples of the most common log file elements that you may need to extract using regex:

Timestamps

Log entries usually contain a timestamp to indicate when an event occurred. Common formats include:

- YYYY-MM-DD HH:MM:SS
- DD/MMM/YYYY:HH:MM:SS +TZ

Regex Pattern:

regex

\d{4}-\d{2}-\d{2} \d{2}:\d{2}:\d{2}

IP Addresses

IP addresses are often included in web server logs, system logs, and security logs. A typical IPv4 address follows the pattern xxx.xxx.xxx.xxx, where xxx is a number from 0 to 255.

Regex Pattern:

regex

(\d{1,3}\.){3}\d{1,3}

HTTP Status Codes

Web server logs often contain HTTP status codes that indicate the result of a client's request. Examples include 200 for success, 404 for "Not Found", and 500 for server errors.

Regex Pattern:

regex

HTTP/\d\.\d" (\d{3})

URLs

Log files may contain URLs representing client requests. These URLs can be extracted to monitor traffic to specific pages or endpoints.

Regex Pattern:

regex

"http[s]?://(?:[a-zA-Z]|[0-9]|[$-_@.&+]|[!*\\(\\),]|(?:%[0-9a-fA-F][0-9a-fA-F]))+"

Error Messages

Error logs and application logs often contain error messages or exception traces. These messages can be identified and parsed using regex.

Regex Pattern:

regex

(?:ERROR|EXCEPTION)\s+\[.*\]\s+(.+)

---

3. Extracting Useful Data from Log Files Using Regex

Once you understand the common patterns in log files, you can start using regex to extract useful data. Below are some real-world examples of how regex can be applied to parse and analyze log files.

---

4. Real-World Example: Analyzing Server Logs for Error Tracking

Imagine you're working as a system administrator or developer, and you need to track errors in the server logs to identify potential issues with your application or server.

Let's say you have a log file that contains lines like the following:

log

2024-12-17 12:05:32 ERROR [Server] Connection timeout while accessing /api/data
2024-12-17 12:06:15 INFO [Server] User logged in with IP 192.168.1.2
2024-12-17 12:07:45 ERROR [Database] Failed to connect to the database at 10.0.0.1
2024-12-17 12:08:02 ERROR [Server] Connection timeout while accessing /api/login

Step 1: Identify Errors
You want to extract the error messages from the log file to track failed connections and other issues. The error entries are typically

marked with the keyword ERROR, and the actual error message follows.

Regex Pattern:

regex

ERROR\s+\[([^\]]+)\]\s+(.+)

This pattern matches the word ERROR, followed by the square brackets containing the source of the error (e.g., Server, Database), and the actual error message.

Code Example:

python

```
import re

log_data = """
2024-12-17 12:05:32 ERROR [Server] Connection timeout while accessing /api/data
2024-12-17 12:06:15 INFO [Server] User logged in with IP 192.168.1.2
2024-12-17 12:07:45 ERROR [Database] Failed to connect to the database at 10.0.0.1
2024-12-17 12:08:02 ERROR [Server] Connection timeout while accessing /api/login
"""

# Regex to find error messages
pattern = r"ERROR\s+\[([^\]]+)\]\s+(.+)"
matches = re.findall(pattern, log_data)
```

```
for match in matches:
    print(f"Error Source: {match[0]}, Message: {match[1]}")
```

Output:

text

Error Source: Server, Message: Connection timeout while accessing /api/data
Error Source: Database, Message: Failed to connect to the database at 10.0.0.1
Error Source: Server, Message: Connection timeout while accessing /api/login

Step 2: Count the Frequency of Errors

You might also want to track how many errors occur in a specific category, such as Server or Database.

Code Example:

python

```python
from collections import Counter

# Count errors by source
error_sources = [match[0] for match in matches]
source_counts = Counter(error_sources)

for source, count in source_counts.items():
    print(f"Error Source: {source}, Count: {count}")
```

Output:

text

Error Source: Server, Count: 2

Error Source: Database, Count: 1

5.

Log file parsing and analysis is a crucial task in maintaining and troubleshooting applications, servers, and systems. By mastering regex patterns, you can efficiently extract, process, and analyze log data. Whether you're tracking errors, auditing system activity, or monitoring performance, regex provides a flexible and powerful solution for automating these tasks.

In this chapter, we've learned how to use regex to identify common patterns in log files, extract useful data, and analyze server logs for error tracking. With the ability to parse and process large amounts of log data quickly and efficiently, regex becomes an indispensable tool for system administrators, developers, and analysts.

In the next chapter, we'll dive into how you can automate the parsing of more complex log files, handle various formats, and perform deeper analyses using Python and regex together.

Chapter 18: Validating User Input with Regex

Validating user input is a critical aspect of web development and data processing. Ensuring that the data entered by users meets specific criteria is essential for preventing errors, security vulnerabilities, and ensuring data integrity. Regular expressions (regex) are a powerful tool for performing validation on various types of user input such as email addresses, phone numbers, and ZIP codes.

In this chapter, we will explore how to use regex for common validation tasks and discuss the importance of pattern matching for checking input correctness. We'll cover the syntax and structure of regex patterns tailored to validate different formats. Additionally, we'll walk through a real-world example of how to use regex to validate a user registration form that includes fields like email addresses, phone numbers, and ZIP codes.

1. Why Input Validation Matters

Input validation is an essential step to ensure that data provided by users adheres to required formats and constraints. In the context of forms and applications, invalid or malicious input can lead to various issues, such as incorrect data, errors, or security vulnerabilities like SQL injection or cross-site scripting (XSS).

2. How Regex Helps with Validation

Regular expressions are well-suited for validating user input because they allow you to define patterns that the data must match. Rather than writing complex conditional statements or looping through characters manually, regex enables you to perform sophisticated checks with a single line of code. You can use regex to ensure that user input matches a specific format or pattern, such as:

- **Email Addresses:** Ensuring the email contains characters before and after the "@" symbol, followed by a valid domain.
- **Phone Numbers:** Matching various phone number formats, whether with dashes, parentheses, or spaces.
- **ZIP Codes:** Validating the format of postal codes, including 5-digit and 9-digit formats in the US.

3. Common User Input Patterns and Their Validation

Here are common regex patterns to validate user input:

Email Address Validation

A regex for validating an email address checks that it contains text before the "@" symbol, followed by a valid domain. The regex pattern for a simple email validation might look like this:

python

```
email_pattern = r"^[a-zA-Z0-9_.+-]+@[a-zA-Z0-9-]+\.[a-zA-Z0-9-.]+$"
```

- **Explanation:**
  - ^[a-zA-Z0-9_.+-]+: The email starts with one or more alphanumeric characters, underscores, periods, pluses, or hyphens.
  - @[a-zA-Z0-9-]+: The "@" symbol is followed by one or more alphanumeric characters or hyphens for the domain.
  - \.[a-zA-Z0-9-.]+$: The domain has a period followed by one or more alphanumeric characters, periods, or hyphens at the end.

Phone Number Validation

A phone number can have various formats: (XXX) XXX-XXXX, XXX-XXX-XXXX, or even XXXXXXXXXX. A regex to validate these formats could look like:

python

```
phone_pattern = r"^(\(\d{3}\)\s?|\d{3}-)\d{3}-\d{4}$"
```

135

- **Explanation:**
  - o (\(\d{3}\)\s?|\d{3}-): Matches the area code, either in parentheses or with dashes.
  - o \d{3}-\d{4}: Matches the local part of the phone number.

ZIP Code Validation

A simple 5-digit ZIP code can be validated with:

python

```
zip_code_pattern = r"^\d{5}$"
```

And for a 9-digit ZIP code with the extended 4 digits:

python

```
zip_code_pattern_extended = r"^\d{5}-\d{4}$"
```

- **Explanation:**
  - o \d{5}: Matches exactly 5 digits.
  - o \d{5}-\d{4}: Matches the 5-digit format followed by a hyphen and 4 more digits.

4. Real-World Example: Validating a User Registration Form

In a real-world scenario, user registration forms need to verify the correctness of user input before saving it to a database or proceeding with account creation. Let's walk through how we can use regex in Python to validate the fields for an email address, phone number, and ZIP code.

python

```python
import re

# Sample user input
user_input = {
    "email": "john.doe@example.com",
    "phone": "(123) 456-7890",
    "zip": "12345-6789"
}

# Regex patterns
email_pattern = r"^[a-zA-Z0-9_.+-]+@[a-zA-Z0-9-]+\.[a-zA-Z0-9-.]+$"
phone_pattern = r"^(\(\d{3}\))\s?|\d{3}-)\d{3}-\d{4}$"
zip_pattern = r"^\d{5}-\d{4}$"

# Validation function
def validate_input(input_data):
    validation_results = {}

    # Validate email
    email_valid = bool(re.match(email_pattern, input_data["email"]))
    validation_results["email"] = "Valid" if email_valid else "Invalid"

    # Validate phone number
    phone_valid = bool(re.match(phone_pattern, input_data["phone"]))
```

```python
    validation_results["phone"] = "Valid" if phone_valid else "Invalid"

    # Validate ZIP code
    zip_valid = bool(re.match(zip_pattern, input_data["zip"]))
    validation_results["zip"] = "Valid" if zip_valid else "Invalid"

    return validation_results

# Check the input
validation_results = validate_input(user_input)
print(validation_results)
```

Output:

python

```
{'email': 'Valid', 'phone': 'Valid', 'zip': 'Valid'}
```

5.

Regex is a powerful tool for validating user input, ensuring that data is correct, consistent, and safe before being used in your application. With just a few lines of code, you can validate common fields like email addresses, phone numbers, and ZIP codes. In the real-world example, we saw how regex helps automate the validation of multiple fields in a user registration form, providing a more efficient and secure approach to input validation.

In the next chapters, we will dive deeper into more advanced applications of regex, such as form validation for more complex inputs, error handling, and processing large datasets efficiently using regex in Python.

Chapter 19: Automating Text Manipulation with Regex in Python

In the world of text processing, there are often situations where you need to modify large sets of text data based on specific patterns. Manual editing can be tedious, time-consuming, and error-prone, especially when working with large files or datasets. This is where automation comes into play. Regular expressions, paired with Python's re.sub() function, allow you to automate text manipulation tasks efficiently and accurately.

In this chapter, we'll dive into how to use re.sub() for text replacement in various scenarios, from simple string replacements to complex pattern-based transformations. You'll learn how to batch replace specific words, characters, or entire patterns across large files, making your text processing tasks much more streamlined and less prone to human error.

1. The Basics of re.sub()

Python's re.sub() function allows you to search for a pattern within a string and replace it with a new string. This function provides a simple and efficient way to perform automated text manipulation.

The basic syntax of re.sub() is:

python

```
import re
re.sub(pattern, replacement, string)
```

- **pattern**: The regular expression pattern you want to search for.
- **replacement**: The string that will replace the matched pattern.
- **string**: The string to be searched and modified.

The function returns a new string with all occurrences of the pattern replaced by the replacement string.

2. Batch Replacing Words or Characters

One common use of re.sub() is to replace certain words or characters in a document or across multiple documents. This can be helpful in scenarios such as data cleaning, formatting corrections, or simply replacing deprecated terminology.

Example: Replacing Incorrect Terms in Text

Imagine you have a text document that contains the word "company" throughout, but you want to replace it with "corporation." You can use re.sub() to replace all instances of "company" with "corporation."

python

```
import re
```

```
text = "Our company has been growing steadily. The company values innovation."
updated_text = re.sub(r'company', 'corporation', text)
print(updated_text)
```

Output:

perl

Our corporation has been growing steadily. The corporation values innovation.
This is a simple example, but re.sub() can be used for more complex replacements, such as replacing variations of a word or handling different case types.

3. Using Groups for Advanced Text Manipulation

In some cases, you may want to replace specific parts of a match while preserving other parts. You can use capturing groups to reference specific sections of the match in the replacement string.

Example: Swapping First and Last Names

Suppose you have a list of names in the format "First Last," and you want to swap them to the format "Last, First." Using capturing groups, you can match the first and last name and then reference them in reverse order.

python

```
import re

text = "John Doe, Alice Smith, Bob Johnson"
```

```
updated_text = re.sub(r'(\w+)\s(\w+)', r'\2, \1', text)
print(updated_text)
```

Output:

Doe, John, Smith, Alice, Johnson, Bob

Here, (\w+) captures the first name, and (\w+) captures the last name. In the replacement string r'\2, \1', \2 refers to the second captured group (last name), and \1 refers to the first captured group (first name).

4. Using re.sub() for Complex Pattern Replacement

Beyond simple word replacement, re.sub() is extremely powerful when dealing with more complex patterns. You can replace based on patterns such as dates, phone numbers, or even HTML tags.

Example: Replacing Date Formats

Suppose you have dates in the format "DD-MM-YYYY" and you want to convert them to "YYYY-MM-DD." You can use regex to match and replace the dates.

python

```
import re

text = "The event is scheduled for 12-05-2022, and the next one is on 15-06-2022."
updated_text = re.sub(r'(\d{2})-(\d{2})-(\d{4})', r'\3-\2-\1', text)
print(updated_text)
```

Output:

vbnet

The event is scheduled for 2022-05-12, and the next one is on 2022-06-15. In this case, the pattern $(\d\{2\})-(\d\{2\})-(\d\{4\})$ captures the day, month, and year of the date, and the replacement r'\3-\2-\1' rearranges them into the desired format.

5. Batch Processing Multiple Files

In real-world scenarios, you may need to apply text manipulation across multiple files. Using re.sub() in combination with Python's file handling methods, you can automate the replacement process across entire directories of text files.

Example: Replacing Terms in Multiple Files

python

```python
import os
import re

directory = 'path/to/files'
for filename in os.listdir(directory):
    if filename.endswith(".txt"):
        with open(os.path.join(directory, filename), 'r') as file:
            content = file.read()

        # Replace all instances of "company" with "corporation"
        updated_content = re.sub(r'company', 'corporation', content)
```

```
with open(os.path.join(directory, filename), 'w') as file:
    file.write(updated_content)
```

This script will iterate through all .txt files in a specified directory, read their content, perform the text replacement, and then write the updated content back to the file.

6. Real-World Example: Text Preprocessing in Data Science

In data science, preprocessing text data is often an essential step before performing any analysis. Whether you are cleaning social media data, customer feedback, or user-generated content, re.sub() can help clean the data by removing unwanted characters, formatting issues, or correcting typos.

Example: Cleaning a Dataset

Imagine you have a dataset with customer reviews containing special characters, extra spaces, and inconsistent formatting. You can use re.sub() to clean the data.

python

```
import re

reviews = ["Great product!!! ", "Poor quality!!", "  Excellent service!!!"]
cleaned_reviews = [re.sub(r'\s+', ' ', re.sub(r'[^\w\s]', '', review)).strip() for review in reviews]
print(cleaned_reviews)
```

Output:

css

['Great product', 'Poor quality', 'Excellent service']

In this chapter, we've explored how to use Python's re.sub() function to automate text manipulation tasks. From simple word replacements to more complex pattern-based transformations, re.sub() allows you to work with text efficiently and accurately. Whether you're cleaning data, automating repetitive tasks, or processing large datasets, regex is an essential tool in your text-processing toolkit. The real-world examples provided here demonstrate how these techniques can be applied across different domains, making text manipulation tasks more manageable and streamlined.

Chapter 20: Regex for Natural Language Processing (NLP)

Natural Language Processing (NLP) is a field of artificial intelligence that focuses on enabling machines to understand and interact with human language. One of the key challenges in NLP is preprocessing text data to extract useful features and remove irrelevant noise. Regular expressions (regex) are incredibly useful in these tasks, allowing for efficient and precise text manipulation. Whether it's removing punctuation, splitting sentences, or cleaning up text for machine learning models, regex can be your most powerful tool in NLP.

In this chapter, we'll explore how regular expressions can be used to preprocess text data for NLP tasks. From basic tokenization to complex cleaning operations, regex enables efficient handling of raw text, which is often messy and unstructured. We will walk through several real-world examples to demonstrate the role of regex in NLP workflows, with a particular focus on how to prepare text for sentiment analysis, one of the most common tasks in NLP.

1. Tokenization with Regex

Tokenization is the process of splitting text into smaller, meaningful units called tokens, such as words, phrases, or symbols. Before performing any NLP task, text must be tokenized to break it down into manageable pieces. Regular expressions are excellent for tokenization because they allow you to define patterns for what constitutes a token.

- **Whitespace tokenization:** A simple approach involves splitting text based on spaces or punctuation. You can use regex to split on spaces while ignoring any leading or trailing whitespace.

python

```
import re
text = "Natural language processing is fun!"
tokens = re.findall(r'\b\w+\b', text)
print(tokens)
# Output: ['Natural', 'language', 'processing', 'is', 'fun']
```

- **Custom tokenization:** You can create more sophisticated tokenization patterns, such as splitting by sentences, handling contractions, or distinguishing between words and punctuation marks.

python

```
text = "I'm learning NLP. It's fun!"
tokens = re.findall(r'\b\w+\b|[^\w\s]', text)
print(tokens)
# Output: ['I', 'm', 'learning', 'NLP', '.', 'It', 's', 'fun', '!']
```

2. Text Cleaning with Regex

Once tokenized, text often contains unwanted characters, such as punctuation, special symbols, and stop words. Cleaning up this data is crucial for many NLP tasks, especially in sentiment analysis, where irrelevant characters could skew the results. Regular expressions can help clean the text by removing unnecessary elements while preserving the meaningful information.

- **Removing punctuation:** You can use regex to remove all punctuation from a text string, leaving only words.

python

```
text = "Hello, world! It's a beautiful day."
cleaned_text = re.sub(r'[^\w\s]', '', text)
print(cleaned_text)
# Output: 'Hello world Its a beautiful day'
```

- **Lowercasing:** Text normalization, such as converting all text to lowercase, is another essential step in cleaning the data. While Python provides str.lower(), regex can also be used in combination for more advanced patterns if needed.

python

```
text = "Hello World!"
cleaned_text = re.sub(r'[A-Z]', lambda x: x.group(0).lower(), text)
print(cleaned_text)
```

```
# Output: 'hello world!'
```

- **Removing stop words:** Stop words (e.g., "the", "and", "is") are frequently used words that don't carry much meaningful information. Regex can be used to remove or filter out stop words from your text.

python

```
stop_words = r'\b(?:the|and|is|to|of)\b'
text = "This is a sample sentence with stop words."
cleaned_text = re.sub(stop_words, '', text)
print(cleaned_text)
# Output: 'This a sample sentence with stop words.'
```

3. Preparing Text for Sentiment Analysis

Sentiment analysis involves determining the sentiment or emotional tone of a piece of text, typically classifying it as positive, negative, or neutral. Before running sentiment analysis algorithms, the text needs to be preprocessed, which often includes removing noise, normalizing text, and ensuring that the relevant information remains intact.

In this section, we'll show how regex can be applied to preprocess data specifically for sentiment analysis.

- **Removing special characters and emojis:** Sentiment analysis models may struggle with emojis, special characters, or other non-text symbols. Regex can be used to remove these elements.

python

```
text = "I love this! ☺ #Amazing"
cleaned_text = re.sub(r'[^\w\s]', '', text)  # Removing punctuation
print(cleaned_text)
# Output: 'I love this Amazing'
```

- **Handling negations:** In sentiment analysis, negation words like "not" or "isn't" can reverse the meaning of a sentence. Regex can help identify negations and handle them properly before analysis.

python

```
text = "I am not happy with the service."
negation_pattern = r'\bnot\b|\bno\b|\bnever\b'  # Example of negation words
cleaned_text = re.sub(negation_pattern, 'NEG', text)
print(cleaned_text)
# Output: 'I am NEG happy with the service.'
```

- **Removing URLs, mentions, and hashtags:** In modern text, URLs, mentions (@username), and hashtags (#topic) are prevalent. For sentiment analysis, these are typically not useful. Regex can be used to filter these elements.

python

```
text = "Check this out! http://example.com #Python @user"
cleaned_text = re.sub(r'https?://\S+|www\.\S+', '', text)  # Remove URLs
cleaned_text = re.sub(r'@\w+', '', cleaned_text)  # Remove mentions
cleaned_text = re.sub(r'#\w+', '', cleaned_text)  # Remove hashtags
print(cleaned_text)
# Output: 'Check this out!'
```

4. Case Study: Preprocessing Text Data for Sentiment Analysis

Let's combine these techniques into a real-world example. Suppose we have a dataset of product reviews and we need to preprocess the text to prepare it for sentiment analysis. The preprocessing pipeline will include tokenization, cleaning, stop word removal, handling negations, and normalizing text.

python

```
import re

# Sample product review
review = "I absolutely love this product! It's the best purchase I've made. #Amazing"

# 1. Remove hashtags, URLs, and mentions
review = re.sub(r'#\w+', '', review)
review = re.sub(r'https?://\S+|www\.\S+', '', review)
```

```
# 2. Remove punctuation
review = re.sub(r'[^\w\s]', '', review)


# 3. Convert to lowercase
review = review.lower()


# 4. Tokenization (basic whitespace-based)
tokens = re.findall(r'\b\w+\b', review)


# 5. Remove stop words
stop_words = r'\b(?:the|and|is|to|of)\b'
review = re.sub(stop_words, '', review)


# 6. Handle negation
review = re.sub(r'\bnot\b|\bno\b|\bnever\b', 'NEG', review)


print("Preprocessed review:", review)
# Output: 'i absolutely love this product its best purchase ive made amazing'
```

Regular expressions play a crucial role in text preprocessing for NLP, especially when working with raw text data that needs to be cleaned, tokenized, or transformed. By mastering regex, you can ensure that your data is properly formatted and ready for further analysis, whether it's for sentiment analysis, machine learning, or any other NLP task. In this chapter, we covered a variety of regex techniques, including tokenization, text cleaning, and preparing data for NLP applications like sentiment analysis. With these skills, you'll be well-equipped to tackle a wide range of text processing challenges in Python.

Chapter 21: Regular Expressions for Data Analytics

Regular expressions (regex) play a vital role in data analytics, especially when it comes to working with unstructured or semi-structured data. In many analytics workflows, raw data needs to be cleaned, parsed, or filtered to extract useful insights. Regex provides a powerful and efficient way to perform these tasks, enabling data analysts to quickly identify patterns, extract information, and manipulate text in large datasets.

In this chapter, we will explore how regular expressions can be applied in various data analytics scenarios. From data pipelines to text mining, regex can help streamline the process of cleaning and transforming data. Whether you're working with survey responses, social media comments, or log data, regex helps you filter out noise, detect patterns, and focus on relevant information. We'll look at practical examples and discuss how regex integrates into analytics workflows.

Key Concepts:

1. **Regex in Data Pipelines**
   - Data pipelines often involve the collection, transformation, and storage of large datasets. Regex can be used in the transformation stage to clean and

preprocess data, ensuring it is in a usable format for further analysis.

o For example, regex can be used to extract relevant fields from unstructured text, identify key patterns in log files, or filter out irrelevant information before applying more advanced analytics techniques.

2. **Text Preprocessing for Analytics**

o Raw data, especially text-based data such as survey responses, customer reviews, or social media comments, may contain a lot of noise, such as irrelevant symbols, typos, or formatting issues.

o Regex can help clean and preprocess this text by removing unwanted characters (e.g., special symbols, excess whitespace), standardizing formats (e.g., date and time), or identifying key terms and entities that are relevant to the analysis.

3. **Pattern Matching for Keyword Search**

o One of the most common use cases for regex in data analytics is keyword searching. Whether you're analyzing survey responses or extracting insights from a corpus of text, regex allows you to search for specific patterns (e.g., keywords, phrases, or regular expressions) to identify relevant data points.

    o   For example, regex can be used to search for specific keywords within text responses to categorize or tag the data.

Real-World Example: Analyzing Survey Data for Specific Keywords

Let's imagine you are analyzing survey data collected from a large group of respondents. The survey includes open-ended questions, and you want to identify responses that mention specific keywords, such as "quality," "service," or "delivery."

Without regex, manually searching through the data would be time-consuming and error-prone. Instead, you can use regular expressions to automate the process of searching for these keywords in the responses. Here's how you might do it:

Step 1: Importing Data and Libraries
First, you'll load the survey data into Python and import the necessary libraries, such as re for regex and pandas for data manipulation.

python

```
import pandas as pd
import re

# Sample survey data (in a pandas DataFrame)
```

```
data = pd.DataFrame({
    'responses': [
        'The quality of the product was great!',
        'I was disappointed with the delivery service.',
        'Service was okay, but the quality could improve.',
        'Delivery took longer than expected.'
    ]
})
```

Step 2: Defining the Regex Pattern

Next, define a regex pattern that matches the keywords you're looking for. For example, you might want to find mentions of the words "quality," "service," or "delivery."

python

```
# Regex pattern to match specific keywords
pattern = r'\b(quality|service|delivery)\b'
```

Here, the \b ensures that we match whole words, not substrings (e.g., it will match "service" but not "services").

Step 3: Searching for Keywords in Responses

Now, use re.search() or re.findall() to search for the keywords in the survey responses.

python

```
# Apply regex to identify responses containing the keywords
data['contains_keyword'] = data['responses'].apply(lambda x: bool(re.search(pattern, x, re.IGNORECASE)))
```

```
# Display the filtered responses
print(data)
```

Output:

mathematica

	responses	contains_keyword
0	The quality of the product was great!	True
1	I was disappointed with the delivery service.	True
2	Service was okay, but the quality could improve.	True
3	Delivery took longer than expected.	True

Step 4: Analyzing the Results

Now, you can easily filter or analyze the responses that contain one or more of the specified keywords. This allows you to quickly identify relevant feedback and perform further analysis, such as sentiment analysis, or categorize the responses.

For instance, you might want to count how often each keyword appears in the responses. Using the re.findall() function, you can extract all occurrences of the keywords:

python

```
# Extracting all matches of keywords in responses
data['keywords_found'] = data['responses'].apply(lambda x: re.findall(pattern, x, re.IGNORECASE))

# Counting the frequency of each keyword
```

```
keyword_count = data['keywords_found'].explode().value_counts()
print(keyword_count)
```

Output:

yaml

```
quality    2
service    2
delivery   2
Name: keywords_found, dtype: int64
```

:

In this chapter, we've demonstrated how regex can be used in data analytics workflows, particularly for searching, extracting, and cleaning text data. By applying regular expressions to survey data, we were able to efficiently search for specific keywords, clean the data, and analyze the results. Regex is a powerful tool for any data analyst, enabling faster, more accurate processing of text data and improving the overall efficiency of data analytics workflows.

Regular expressions in Python, particularly with the re library, can help streamline the entire data pipeline, from data collection to preprocessing and analysis, making it an essential skill for anyone working in data analytics.

Chapter 22: Regular Expressions in Data Science

In the world of data science, the process of cleaning and preparing data for analysis is just as important as the analysis itself. Data often comes in raw, unstructured formats, and one of the most common tasks is transforming this data into a structured form that can be analyzed effectively. Regular expressions (regex) provide a powerful toolkit for data scientists to preprocess, clean, and manipulate text-based data, which forms a significant portion of many datasets.

In this chapter, we will explore how regular expressions can be seamlessly integrated into data science workflows. Specifically, we'll cover how regex can assist in cleaning raw data, feature engineering, and preprocessing textual data for various machine learning models. By the end of this chapter, you'll understand how to leverage regex to handle complex text-processing tasks in data science projects and use it as part of your broader data analysis strategy.

---

1. Integrating Regex into Data Science Projects

In data science, one of the most common use cases for regex is data cleaning. Whether you are working with natural language data or any other form of textual information, the ability to identify patterns and extract meaningful insights is crucial.

Data Preprocessing

Before you can use machine learning algorithms or any form of statistical analysis, your data often needs to be cleaned and formatted correctly. This may include:

- Removing or replacing unwanted characters (e.g., HTML tags, special symbols).
- Extracting specific substrings from large text fields (e.g., extracting dates, locations, or product IDs).
- Validating and standardizing values (e.g., ensuring proper formatting for emails or phone numbers).

In each of these tasks, regular expressions provide an efficient, concise way to manipulate text data. For example, cleaning a column that contains messy product descriptions or filtering specific keywords can often be done with just a few lines of regex code.

Feature Engineering

Feature engineering is an essential step in preparing data for machine learning. Regex can help in transforming raw data into more usable features. For instance, you might use regex to extract specific patterns such as:

- **Product categories** from descriptions (e.g., "electronics", "clothing").

- **Text length** or the number of certain characters (e.g., the frequency of certain words in a customer review).

- **Sentiment-related keywords** (e.g., positive or negative sentiment words).

These features can then be used as inputs to machine learning models, improving predictive performance and providing more insights for analysis.

2. Real-World Example: Preprocessing Product Descriptions for a Recommendation Engine

Let's explore a real-world example where we apply regex to preprocess product descriptions for use in a recommendation engine. In an e-commerce environment, product descriptions can be highly variable—ranging from detailed product specifications to short, vague entries. By using regex to standardize and extract relevant information, we can better prepare the data for feature extraction and subsequent analysis.

Scenario:

Suppose you are building a recommendation engine for an online marketplace that sells a wide range of products. The goal is to recommend similar products based on customer preferences. To build the recommendation engine, you need to preprocess and extract useful features from product descriptions, which are often unstructured.

Step 1: Extract Key Product Features Using Regex

- **Example Pattern:** Product descriptions may contain specific product features such as size, color, brand, and price.
- **Regex Solution:** Use regex to match keywords like "size:", "color:", "brand:", and "price:" in the descriptions and extract corresponding values.

python

```
import re

# Sample product description
description = "This red Adidas T-shirt is available in sizes S, M, L. Price: $25"

# Regex pattern to extract size and price
pattern = r"size:\s*([A-Za-z0-9, ]+)|price:\s*\$([0-9]+)"

matches = re.findall(pattern, description)

# Print extracted features
print(matches)
```

Output:

python

[('S, M, L', ''), ('', '25')]

In this case, the regex successfully extracted the product sizes and price. We can use similar regex patterns to capture other key details.

Step 2: Remove Unwanted Data

Product descriptions may also contain irrelevant data such as HTML tags or special characters. Before using the product descriptions in the recommendation engine, you need to clean the text.

- **Regex Solution:** Remove HTML tags using the following pattern:

python

```
html_content = "<div>Buy the best red T-shirt <b>now</b> at a great price!</div>"
cleaned_text = re.sub(r'<.*?>', '', html_content)
print(cleaned_text)
```

Output:

python

Buy the best red T-shirt now at a great price!

Step 3: Tokenize Text for Feature Extraction

Next, you may want to tokenize the product description into individual words or phrases for feature extraction, which can then be used in the recommendation engine.

- **Regex Solution:** Tokenize the text by splitting it into words, removing stop words, and possibly identifying key terms that can be used for categorization.

python

```
description = "This red Adidas T-shirt is available in sizes S, M, L. Price: $25"
tokens = re.findall(r'\b\w+\b', description.lower())
print(tokens)
```

Output:

python

```
['this', 'red', 'adidas', 'tshirt', 'is', 'available', 'in', 'sizes', 's', 'm', 'l', 'price', '25']
```

Step 4: Extract Sentiment or Keywords

In some cases, you may want to identify whether a product description contains sentiment-driven keywords (e.g., "best", "cheap", "luxury"). Regex can be used to detect specific sentiment words within product descriptions.

python

```
# Sentiment-related keywords
sentiment_keywords = ['best', 'cheap', 'luxury', 'high-quality']
```

```
pattern = r'\b(?:' + '|'.join(sentiment_keywords) + r')\b'
sentiment_matches = re.findall(pattern, description.lower())
print(sentiment_matches)
```

Output:

python

['best']

---

3. Integrating Preprocessed Data into a Machine Learning Pipeline

Once the data has been cleaned and features extracted using regex, the next step is to integrate these features into a machine learning pipeline. For instance, the extracted product attributes (such as size, price, or brand) can be used as features for building recommendation models using collaborative filtering or content-based filtering techniques.

Feature Vectorization

The extracted features (e.g., brand, price, and size) might need to be vectorized before they can be used in machine learning models. Techniques like one-hot encoding or TF-IDF vectorization can be used to transform these features into numerical vectors that can be fed into the recommendation system.

Regular expressions are an invaluable tool in the data scientist's toolkit, especially when working with text-based data. They allow you to efficiently clean, transform, and extract relevant information from raw data, which is critical for building effective machine learning models. In this chapter, we've seen how regex can be applied to preprocess product descriptions for a recommendation engine, but the same principles can be extended to a wide variety of use cases in data science.

By mastering regex, data scientists can streamline their data preparation process, improve feature engineering, and enhance their ability to work with complex datasets—ultimately leading to better insights and more accurate models.

Chapter 23: Regex for Software Development

Regular expressions (regex) are not only valuable for text processing tasks in data science and data cleaning but also have a crucial role in software development. As a developer, you often need to work with code, configurations, and text-based inputs, where regex can help you parse, manipulate, and extract valuable information. By incorporating regex into your development toolkit, you can automate tasks, ensure code quality, and enhance your efficiency when working with large codebases or logs.

In this chapter, we will dive into practical uses of regex in the realm of software development. We will focus on tasks like searching for code patterns, extracting specific parts of source code, and validating input data. You will learn how regex can be applied to automate repetitive tasks in development workflows and improve code management.

Key Topics:

1. **Parsing and Searching Code**
   - Developers often need to parse or search through code for specific patterns. Regex is an ideal tool to search for function definitions, variable assignments,

class declarations, or even specific code snippets within larger codebases.

- o Example: Searching for function definitions in Python code files. Regex can be used to identify functions defined using the def keyword, extracting their names, parameters, and even checking for proper docstrings or other annotations.

2. **Code Validation with Regex**

- o Regex can be used to validate code snippets or configuration files. For example, ensuring that a specific coding style is followed, validating regular expression patterns in configuration files, or checking the consistency of indentation and formatting.

- o Example: Use regex to verify that all function definitions in Python adhere to a certain naming convention or structure.

Chapter 24: Regex in Unit Testing

Unit testing is a fundamental part of ensuring the quality and reliability of software. In software development, regex patterns are frequently used to validate input data, process strings, and match specific formats. However, just like any other piece of code, regex patterns themselves should also be tested to ensure they perform as expected in various scenarios. This chapter explores how to write unit tests for regex patterns, validating their correctness and ensuring they handle edge cases and invalid input appropriately.

We'll look at how to integrate regex tests into a unit testing framework, such as Python's built-in unittest library, and provide examples of testing regex patterns. By the end of this chapter, you'll understand how to write, organize, and execute unit tests for regex operations to maintain robust and reliable code.

Key Topics:

1. **Why Regex Needs Unit Testing**
   - The importance of ensuring regex patterns behave as expected.
   - The potential pitfalls of untested regex patterns: false positives, false negatives, and unexpected behavior.
   - Common testing scenarios: validating formats, boundary conditions, and edge cases.
2. **Setting Up Unit Testing for Regex in Python**

o Introduction to Python's unittest framework.

o Basic structure of a unit test in Python.

o How to write and organize unit tests for regex patterns.

3. **Testing Regex Match and Search Functions**

o Writing tests to check for matches (re.match()), searches (re.search()), and all matches (re.findall()).

o Asserting correct results with expected values and handling different input cases.

4. **Real-world Example: Creating Unit Tests for Phone Number Validation Regex**

o **Problem**: You need to validate a string input for phone numbers in a specific format (e.g., 123-456-7890).

o **Regex Pattern**: r"^\d{3}-\d{3}-\d{4}$"

o **Test Cases**:

   ▪ Valid phone numbers (e.g., 123-456-7890).

   ▪ Invalid formats (e.g., 1234567890, 123-45-6789).

   ▪ Edge cases (e.g., empty strings, numbers with extra spaces).

5. **Using Assertions to Validate Test Results**

o Using assertEqual(), assertTrue(), assertFalse(), and other assertion methods in unittest.

o How to compare regex matches with expected output.

o Verifying match results for boundary conditions (e.g., matching exactly three digits and the dash).

6. **Handling Edge Cases in Regex Unit Testing**

o How to handle special characters, whitespace, and unexpected input.

o Writing tests for regex patterns to check how they handle edge cases such as empty input, multiple consecutive dashes, or missing digits.

7. **Example Test Suite for Regex-based Phone Number Validation**

python

```
import unittest
import re

def validate_phone_number(phone_number):
    return bool(re.match(r"^\d{3}-\d{3}-\d{4}$", phone_number))

class TestPhoneNumberValidation(unittest.TestCase):

    def test_valid_phone_number(self):
        self.assertTrue(validate_phone_number("123-456-7890"))

    def test_invalid_phone_number_no_dash(self):
        self.assertFalse(validate_phone_number("1234567890"))

    def test_invalid_phone_number_missing_digit(self):
        self.assertFalse(validate_phone_number("123-45-6789"))
```

```
def test_invalid_phone_number_extra_space(self):
    self.assertFalse(validate_phone_number("123 - 456 - 7890"))

def test_empty_phone_number(self):
    self.assertFalse(validate_phone_number(""))

def test_phone_number_with_special_characters(self):
    self.assertFalse(validate_phone_number("123-456-78@0"))

if __name__ == '__main__':
    unittest.main()
```

- o **Explanation**: This test suite uses Python's unittest framework to test the validate_phone_number() function that checks if a phone number matches a regex pattern. Each test case validates the expected behavior of the regex pattern, including valid and invalid cases.

8. **Best Practices for Testing Regex**
   - o Write tests for expected matches and non-matches.
   - o Consider performance when testing regex for large datasets.
   - o Always test edge cases and ensure regex is working in different environments or locales.

9. **Bonus: Using Regular Expressions in Integration and Functional Testing**

o How to apply regex patterns within larger software tests.

o Integrating regex validation into forms, data inputs, and user interfaces during testing.

:

In this chapter, you've learned the importance of testing regex patterns within your software. You now know how to write unit tests to ensure your regex patterns perform correctly, handle various edge cases, and validate inputs with confidence. By incorporating regex unit testing into your development process, you ensure that your code is robust, reliable, and free from unexpected bugs related to string manipulation and pattern matching.

The ability to efficiently validate regex patterns using unit tests is a key part of mastering regular expressions in Python, and it will make your code more maintainable and resilient to change. Whether you're working on input validation, text processing, or any other regex-based task, unit tests will help you achieve higher-quality code.

Chapter 25: Regex for File and Directory Operations

Regex is a powerful tool that can be used not only for text processing within documents but also for performing complex operations on files and directories. In this chapter, we will explore how regex can help you search, filter, and manipulate files and directories efficiently. Whether you are organizing files, renaming files in bulk, or extracting specific file information based on patterns, regex can significantly enhance your productivity.

Key Topics:

1. **Using Regex for File Searching**
    o   Regex can be used to search for files based on specific naming patterns. For example, if you need to find all files with a certain extension (like .txt or .csv) or all files that follow a particular naming convention, regex makes it easy to filter through large directories.
    o   We'll cover the basics of using the os and re modules in Python to search through file names, including how to write regex patterns that match specific file types or formats.

2. **File Renaming with Regex**
    o   One of the most common use cases for regex in file operations is renaming files. Regex allows you to

write flexible rules for renaming files in bulk, based on patterns in the existing names.

o We'll demonstrate how to use regex to find and replace parts of file names, such as removing underscores, replacing spaces with hyphens, or adding timestamps to files. For example, if you have a set of image files with names like image_01.jpg, image_02.jpg, and so on, regex can help rename them in a more structured format like img_01.jpg, img_02.jpg, etc.

3. **Filtering Files Based on Metadata**

   o Regex can also be used to filter files based on metadata, such as the file creation date or modification date, by combining it with other Python modules like os or glob.

   o We'll look at how to construct regex patterns that match file attributes, such as certain ranges of dates or specific patterns in metadata.

4. **Real-World Example: Renaming Files in a Directory Using Regex**

   o In this real-world example, we'll explore how to use regex to rename a batch of files in a directory. This might include tasks like:

     ▪ Cleaning up file names to remove unwanted characters.

- Renaming files according to a consistent naming convention.
- Automatically numbering files in a specific order (e.g., image_001.jpg, image_002.jpg).

Example Code for Renaming Files:

python

```
import os
import re

# Directory where files are located
directory = '/path/to/your/directory'

# Regex pattern to find and rename files (e.g., replacing spaces with underscores)
pattern = r'(\s+)'  # Match any whitespace
replacement = '_'

for filename in os.listdir(directory):
    if re.search(pattern, filename):  # Check if the filename matches the pattern
        new_filename = re.sub(pattern, replacement, filename) # Rename the file
        os.rename(os.path.join(directory, filename), os.path.join(directory, new_filename))
        print(f'Renamed: {filename} -> {new_filename}')
```

In the above example:

- o We use the re.search() function to check if a file name contains spaces (or any whitespace).
- o If the pattern is matched, re.sub() replaces spaces with underscores, and the file is renamed using os.rename().

5. **Advanced File Operations with Regex**

- o Once you're comfortable with basic file searching and renaming, you can extend your regex skills to more advanced file operations, such as batch renaming based on a set of rules, or searching for files that match multiple patterns.
- o Additionally, regex can help when parsing file contents, for example, to identify specific sections within log files, or parsing data from a collection of documents.

Real-World Example:

Imagine you work in a data science team and regularly receive raw data files with inconsistent naming conventions, such as data_01.csv, data-02.csv, DATA_03.csv. You need to organize them into a more standardized format such as data_001.csv, data_002.csv, data_003.csv. This can be achieved easily using regex for renaming files systematically in Python.

Best Practices for File Operations with Regex:

- **Be cautious when renaming files:** It's essential to ensure your regex patterns are thoroughly tested before applying them to many files, as incorrect patterns can result in file names that are difficult to undo.

- **Use backups:** Before performing bulk operations like renaming or moving files, it is always a good idea to back up the original files to avoid data loss.

- **Testing with a smaller set:** Always test your regex patterns on a small subset of files first to verify that they work as expected.

:

In this chapter, we've explored how regex can make your work with files and directories more efficient and organized. Whether you're managing data files, performing bulk renaming, or filtering files based on specific patterns, regex can automate and simplify the task. With the knowledge gained here, you can confidently tackle file-based operations in your projects and workflows.

Chapter 26: Regex for Handling HTML and XML

HTML and XML are markup languages widely used in web development and data exchange. They are both structured in a hierarchical way, making them ideal for representing data with different levels of information. While specialized libraries like BeautifulSoup or lxml are typically preferred for parsing and navigating HTML and XML documents, regex can still be a valuable tool in some scenarios. In this chapter, we'll explore how to use regular expressions to handle and extract information from HTML and XML data efficiently.

Key Topics:

1. **Challenges of Using Regex with HTML/XML**
    o   Regex is not inherently designed to parse hierarchical data like HTML or XML, which can present challenges such as handling nested tags and different tag structures. We'll explain why this can be difficult and how to overcome some of these challenges using regex.

2. **Using Regex for Extracting HTML/XML Data**
    o   While regex is not the ideal solution for complex HTML/XML parsing, it can be effective for simple tasks like extracting certain patterns or specific

content. Common tasks might include extracting product prices, links, or titles from HTML pages. We'll cover how regex can be used in these cases.

- o Example patterns include:
  - Extracting all <a> tags (links) from an HTML page.
  - Extracting text between specific tags (like <title>, <h1>, or <p>).
  - Extracting product prices embedded in HTML with specific classes or IDs.

3. **Real-World Example: Parsing Product Prices from an HTML Page**

  - o In a real-world scenario, we may want to extract product prices from an e-commerce website. While using a dedicated web scraping library like BeautifulSoup would be ideal, regex can still be used effectively when you know the structure of the HTML.

  - o **Example**: We are given a product listing HTML page, and we need to extract all prices listed next to product names. The prices are in <span> tags with the class price. The following regex pattern can help us find the prices:

    python

```python
import re

html_content = '''
<html>
  <body>
    <div class="product">
      <span class="name">Product 1</span>
      <span class="price">$49.99</span>
    </div>
    <div class="product">
      <span class="name">Product 2</span>
      <span class="price">$29.99</span>
    </div>
  </body>
</html>
'''

# Regex to extract prices from the HTML content
pattern = r'<span class="price">(\$\d+\.\d{2})</span>'
prices = re.findall(pattern, html_content)

print(prices)  # Output: ['$49.99', '$29.99']
```

o **Explanation**:

- The regex pattern `<span class="price">(\$\d+\.\d{2})</span>` is designed to match prices inside <span> tags with the class price.

- \$\d+\.\d{2} matches the price format, ensuring it starts with a dollar sign and includes two decimal places (e.g., $49.99).

4. **Handling Edge Cases in HTML/XML Parsing**

   o Although regex can work for simple patterns in HTML/XML, it can break when dealing with more complex structures, such as nested tags or varying attributes. We'll discuss some strategies for dealing with edge cases, like ensuring that a price is properly extracted from a tag even if extra spaces or nested elements are present.

   o Example: Handling extra spaces or additional nested tags inside the <span> element.

python

```
html_content = '''
<html>
  <body>
    <div class="product">
      <span class="price"> <b>$49.99</b> </span>
    </div>
  </body>
</html>
'''

# Adjusting the regex pattern to handle extra spaces and nested tags
pattern = r'<span class="price">\s*<b>(\$\d+\.\d{2})</b>\s*</span>'
```

```
prices = re.findall(pattern, html_content)
```

```
print(prices)  # Output: ['$49.99']
```

5. **When to Avoid Regex for HTML/XML Parsing**

   o While regex can work well for specific tasks, it's important to know when to avoid it. If the HTML/XML structure is complex or deeply nested, regex can become error-prone and difficult to manage. In such cases, we recommend using specialized libraries like BeautifulSoup (for HTML) or lxml (for both XML and HTML) that provide a more robust and reliable way to parse these documents.

6. **Best Practices for Using Regex with HTML/XML**

   o Always be cautious when using regex to parse HTML/XML. Regular expressions can quickly become complex and difficult to maintain, especially with malformed or unpredictable input.

   o Ensure that you test your regex patterns thoroughly to account for variations in the HTML/XML structure (e.g., extra spaces, nested tags).

   o Use regex for simple and repetitive tasks like extracting specific tags, but switch to a full-fledged HTML/XML parser for anything more complex.

:

In this chapter, we've covered how to use regular expressions to extract data from HTML and XML documents. While regex is not the best tool for parsing complex or deeply nested structures, it can be quite effective for extracting specific information such as links, prices, or dates from HTML pages. By combining regex with Python's powerful libraries like re, we can streamline tasks such as web scraping and data extraction. However, for more complex or hierarchical structures, it's essential to consider using specialized parsers for more reliable and efficient results.

In the next chapter, we will look into how to use regex for more advanced text manipulation tasks, including replacing and reformatting content within HTML or XML files.

Chapter 27: Advanced Regex Challenges

Regular expressions (regex) are incredibly powerful, but as patterns become more complex, so too does the challenge of writing, debugging, and maintaining them. Advanced regex tasks often involve handling intricate, multi-line text, managing nested structures, or matching patterns that span multiple lines of input. In this chapter, we'll explore some advanced regex challenges, offer techniques for troubleshooting tricky patterns, and provide real-world examples to help you master these challenges.

Key Topics:

1. **Handling Complex and Multi-Line Text**
   - **Challenges with multi-line text**: Regular expressions traditionally work on single lines, but real-world scenarios often involve multi-line strings, such as logs, HTML content, or structured text that spans several lines. We'll dive into how to handle these situations using regex, including the re.DOTALL flag for matching across line breaks.
   - **Real-world example**: Matching and extracting structured data, such as log entries or email bodies, from a multi-line text.

2. **Working with Nested Patterns**

- o **Nested structures**: One of the most difficult tasks in regex is handling nested or recursive patterns, such as matching parentheses, HTML/XML tags, or JSON objects. While regex is not inherently designed for recursive parsing, there are techniques and workarounds to handle these scenarios.

- o **Real-world example**: Extracting balanced parentheses or HTML tags, handling both opening and closing tags within the same input.

3. **Regex Debugging and Troubleshooting**

- o **Common pitfalls**: Regex can easily become unreadable or overly complicated. Issues like infinite loops, unintentional greedy matches, or performance problems can arise. In this section, we'll provide tips on how to debug and troubleshoot regex patterns to ensure they behave as expected.

- o **Tools for debugging**: Introduction to various online regex testing tools like regex101 and regexr, which allow you to test regex patterns, view matches, and receive instant feedback.

- o **Real-world example**: Debugging a pattern designed to extract email addresses from a large text file, identifying problems such as missing or incorrect matches.

4. **Performance Considerations**

o **Regex performance issues**: As regex patterns grow more complex, they can become computationally expensive, especially when working with large datasets or text files. We'll look into best practices for optimizing regex performance, including efficient use of quantifiers, anchors, and other performance-enhancing techniques.

o **Real-world example**: Optimizing a regex pattern used to search a large server log for error codes, improving search speed without sacrificing accuracy.

5. **Advanced Pattern Matching Techniques**

o **Lookaheads and Lookbehinds**: These are powerful but often misunderstood components of regex. We'll dive deeper into using positive and negative lookaheads and lookbehinds to match conditions before or after a certain pattern, without consuming characters in the input.

o **Real-world example**: Using lookahead to match a sequence of digits that must appear before a certain character, such as extracting version numbers from text.

Real-World Example: Matching and Extracting Data from Complex, Multi-Line Text

Consider the following task: you're tasked with parsing log files from a web server, and you need to extract specific error messages, timestamps, and user IPs. These logs can span multiple lines, with each entry having varying formats.

Here's how you could approach this challenge:

1. **Multi-line Matching**:
   o Logs often span multiple lines, and regex by default matches only within a single line. To match across multiple lines, you would use the re.DOTALL flag.

python

```
import re
log_data = "'[INFO] 2021-07-01 12:00:00 User 123.45.67.89 accessed
the page.
[ERROR] 2021-07-01 12:01:00 Server error occurred.
[INFO] 2021-07-01 12:05:00 User 987.65.43.21 accessed the page.'"

# Regex to match log entries across lines
pattern = r"\[ERROR\].*?(\d{4}-\d{2}-\d{2})\s(\d{2}:\d{2}:\d{2})"
matches = re.findall(pattern, log_data, re.DOTALL)
print(matches)  # Outputs: [('2021-07-01', '12:01:00')]
```

2. **Handling Nested Structures**:
   o If you need to extract data within nested structures (e.g., matching content inside tags), you would have to use careful lookahead and lookbehind assertions or split the matching into multiple stages.

python

```
log_data = '''<log>
<entry><date>2021-07-01</date><error>404</error></entry>
<entry><date>2021-07-02</date><error>500</error></entry>
</log>'''

# Match error codes inside XML-like tags
pattern = r"<error>(\d{3})</error>"
matches = re.findall(pattern, log_data)
print(matches)  # Outputs: ['404', '500']
```

3. **Debugging Regex Patterns**:
   - o Debugging regex can be difficult when the pattern doesn't behave as expected. By using tools like regex101, you can analyze why a match fails or behaves unexpectedly, and adjust your pattern accordingly.
   - o **Example**: If you're trying to match an email but your pattern is erroneously matching extra characters, regex101 can highlight exactly where your pattern went wrong (e.g., not accounting for the period or the plus sign in the username).

4. **Performance Optimization**:
   - o For large datasets, regex patterns can slow down, especially if they are overly complex or improperly structured. By using anchors (^ and $), limiting

backtracking, and simplifying quantifiers, you can ensure your regex operates efficiently on large text files.

python

```
pattern = r"^(ERROR|INFO)\s(\d{4}-\d{2}-\d{2})"
# Anchors at the start (^) and end ($) of the line reduce unnecessary backtracking.
```

By the end of this chapter, you will have learned how to tackle the most advanced regex challenges you might encounter in real-world text processing tasks. You'll also have the tools and strategies to debug, optimize, and refine your regex patterns, making your code faster, more efficient, and easier to maintain.

Chapter 28: Regex Best Practices

Regular expressions (regex) are a powerful tool, but their complexity can quickly escalate as patterns become more advanced. Writing efficient, maintainable, and readable regex patterns is crucial, especially in production environments. In this chapter, we will explore best practices for writing regex, strategies for debugging and optimizing regex patterns, and how to avoid common pitfalls that can lead to inefficient or buggy expressions.

We'll also walk through a real-world example of refactoring a complex regex pattern to improve both its performance and readability.

Key Topics:

1. **Writing Efficient and Maintainable Regex Patterns**
   - **Keep it Simple**: Start with the simplest regex pattern that solves the problem and then refine it. Avoid overly complex patterns unless absolutely necessary.
   - **Use Specific Character Classes**: Instead of using broad character classes like . (which matches any character), narrow down the scope using specific character classes (e.g., \d for digits, \w for word characters).

o **Avoid Excessive Backtracking**: When crafting regex patterns, excessive backtracking can lead to poor performance, especially with large datasets. For example, patterns that match large sets of characters with greedy quantifiers (.*) can cause excessive backtracking. Using non-greedy quantifiers (.*?) or more specific matches can often mitigate this.

o **Group for Clarity and Reusability**: Use grouping to isolate distinct portions of your regex pattern. This improves readability and allows you to reuse parts of the pattern through backreferences.

o **Anchor Your Matches**: Where possible, use anchors (^ for the start, $ for the end) to limit where your pattern matches. Anchors improve performance by narrowing the search scope.

2. **Debugging Regex Patterns**

o **Regex Testing Tools**: Use online tools like regex101.com or regexr.com to test your regular expressions. These tools provide real-time feedback, highlighting which part of the regex pattern is causing a match failure and suggesting improvements.

o **Unit Testing for Regex**: Incorporating unit tests for regex patterns helps ensure that they work as expected across various edge cases. For instance, testing a phone number validation pattern against a variety of input formats (valid, invalid, edge cases).

o **Check for Overlaps**: When debugging, ensure that your regex is not accidentally matching unintended strings. Overlapping matches can lead to unexpected behavior, so carefully evaluate how your regex behaves with different inputs.

o **Break Down Complex Patterns**: If you have a complex regex pattern, break it down into smaller, more manageable parts. Testing each part individually can help isolate any issues.

3. **Avoiding Common Pitfalls**

o **Avoid Greedy Quantifiers**: As mentioned earlier, greedy quantifiers (*, +, {m,}) can cause issues like excessive backtracking, which can drastically reduce performance, particularly in long strings. Prefer lazy quantifiers (*?, +?, {m,n}?) to match the shortest possible string.

o **Repetitive Patterns**: Avoid writing repetitive or overly specific patterns that are harder to maintain. For example, a regex pattern to match a date in various formats might be written more efficiently using pre-built classes or libraries rather than creating a custom solution.

MASTERING REGEX WITH PYTHON

o **Performance Concerns**: Regex is powerful, but it's not always the fastest tool for every job. When performance is a concern (e.g., processing massive logs), sometimes using built-in string methods or other tools in conjunction with regex can be a more optimal solution.

4. **Real-World Example: Refactoring a Complex Regex Pattern** Let's take a complex regex pattern and refactor it for readability and performance.

Before Refactoring:

python

```
import re

text = "Order number: 12345, Date: 2021-06-15, Status: Shipped"
pattern = r"Order number: (\d+), Date: (\d{4}-\d{2}-\d{2}), Status: (\w+)"
result = re.search(pattern, text)

if result:
    print(result.groups())
```

In this example, the pattern is already functional, but let's make some adjustments:

o **Clarify Grouping**: We can improve the clarity of the pattern by adding non-capturing groups where appropriate and using anchors to make the pattern more specific.

- o **Optimize the Date Format**: The date format could be made more flexible without using repetitive character classes.

After Refactoring:

python

```
import re

text = "Order number: 12345, Date: 2021-06-15, Status: Shipped"
pattern = r"^Order number: (\d+), Date: (\d{4}-\d{2}-\d{2}), Status: (\w+)$"
result = re.search(pattern, text)

if result:
    print(f"Order Number: {result.group(1)}")
    print(f"Date: {result.group(2)}")
    print(f"Status: {result.group(3)}")
```

- o **Anchors for Precision**: By adding ^ at the start and $ at the end, we ensure that the pattern matches the entire string, reducing the chance of partial matches.
- o **Improved Grouping**: Instead of capturing groups unnecessarily, we could also consider non-capturing groups (?:...) for optional parts of the pattern to improve performance if needed.

This refactored version improves readability and ensures the pattern is more maintainable and precise, especially when working with structured data.

Mastering regex involves not only understanding the syntax but also applying best practices for efficiency, maintainability, and debugging. By following these best practices, developers can write regex patterns that are both effective and easy to understand, making them valuable tools for text manipulation, data cleaning, and validation tasks. Remember, regex is powerful, but simplicity and clarity are key to avoiding errors and ensuring the longevity of your code.

In this chapter, we've covered techniques for writing efficient and maintainable regex, common pitfalls to avoid, and strategies for debugging regex patterns. Through our real-world example, you can see how refactoring a complex regex pattern can improve both its readability and performance, making it more robust and easier to maintain in the future.

Chapter 29: The Future of Regex in Python

Regular expressions (regex) have been an essential part of text processing and data manipulation for decades, especially in programming languages like Python. With their ability to match patterns in strings, they provide an efficient solution to a wide array of problems ranging from simple search and replace tasks to complex data extraction. However, like all technologies, regex is evolving, with new trends and capabilities emerging that expand its applications even further.

In this chapter, we will explore the future of regex in Python, including advancements in regex engines, emerging trends that influence how we use regex, and the increasing role regex will play in the context of automation, artificial intelligence (AI), and machine learning (ML). We will also look at the potential developments in the Python ecosystem that could change how we approach regex-based tasks and improve its performance and integration in modern development environments.

Key Topics:

1. **Emerging Trends and New Features in Regex Engines**

- o **Performance Improvements**: As systems become more complex and data volumes increase, regex engines are evolving to offer better performance. Optimizations in regex engines, such as Just-In-Time (JIT) compilation and parallelization, are starting to see widespread adoption, making regex more scalable for large datasets.

- o **Support for Named Capture Groups and Extended Syntax**: Modern regex engines are introducing advanced features like named capture groups and enhanced syntax, which simplify complex patterns. Python's re library has already introduced named groups, making it easier to handle complex matches without relying on numbered groups, improving readability and maintainability.

- o **Unicode and Multilingual Matching**: With the increasing globalization of technology, regex engines are improving their support for Unicode and multilingual text processing. This will allow regex to be even more powerful in handling text data in various languages, especially as businesses and tools become more globally focused.

2. **The Evolving Role of Regex in Python Development**
    - o **Integration with Data Science and Machine Learning**: As Python is increasingly used in fields

like data science and AI, regex is being integrated into more data preprocessing tasks, especially when handling messy, unstructured, or semi-structured data. Regex can help clean and preprocess textual data for machine learning models, making it an invaluable tool for feature engineering and data pipeline workflows.

o **Regex for Automation**: With the rise of automation, regex is playing a central role in tasks like log analysis, text extraction from documents, and even code quality checks. As automation tools such as robotic process automation (RPA) become more sophisticated, regex will remain at the core for text-based decision-making, allowing automated systems to read, interpret, and process vast amounts of text data more efficiently.

o **AI-Powered Regex**: One of the emerging trends is the combination of regex with AI-driven tools. Machine learning models can be trained to suggest or generate regex patterns based on examples or the context of the text data. This will simplify the learning curve for developers and help automate the creation of regex patterns for even the most complex tasks.

3. **Real-World Example: Predicting the Future Use of Regex in Automation and AI-Powered Tools**

   o **Use Case 1: Automating Document Processing**: As businesses continue to digitize their operations, the need for automated document processing grows. Regex, combined with AI, could play a huge role in automating the extraction of structured data (like financial information, customer details, etc.) from unstructured text documents (e.g., PDFs, emails, or contracts). AI-powered regex could generate context-sensitive patterns to extract valuable data from a variety of document types.

   o **Use Case 2: Intelligent Web Scraping**: Web scraping has always been a popular use case for regex, but as websites become more dynamic and complex, AI could help automate the process of identifying and extracting relevant data from web pages. Regex will likely be integrated with machine learning models that adapt based on the structure of the web page, improving scraping accuracy and minimizing manual configuration of patterns.

   o **Use Case 3: Real-Time Text Analysis in AI Chatbots**: Regex has been a key component in pattern matching for chatbots, particularly for understanding and processing user input. The future of chatbots will likely involve a more seamless integration of regex with natural language processing (NLP) and AI. Regex will help to identify specific patterns or keywords in user queries while AI models will provide context-aware responses.

4. **Potential Developments in Python's Regex Ecosystem**

   o **Regex Libraries in Python**: Python's re module has been around for a long time, but libraries like regex (a third-party module) offer additional features such as full Unicode support and advanced lookaround assertions. These third-party libraries may become more widely adopted, and Python's built-in re module may evolve to incorporate some of these features, making regex handling even more versatile.

   o **Machine Learning for Regex Generation**: As the role of AI continues to grow, we can expect machine learning models to assist in generating regex patterns automatically. With tools such as regex auto-generation from a set of example strings or data, developers could be freed from manually crafting complex expressions, reducing human error and speeding up the development process.

   o **Integrating Regex with Big Data and Distributed Systems**: As data grows in scale, the need for distributed regex processing in big data environments will grow. Libraries and systems could emerge that allow for the distributed processing of regex patterns over large datasets, perhaps leveraging tools like Apache Spark or Dask in Python. This will be crucial for processing enormous logs or datasets where regex needs to be applied across multiple nodes in a cluster.

: The Future of Regex in Python Development

The future of regex in Python looks bright, with continuous advancements in performance, usability, and integration with cutting-edge technologies. While regex has been a staple in text processing for years, its role will expand and evolve as Python continues to serve as the language of choice in emerging fields like data science, AI, and automation.

As regex engines become smarter, and machine learning and AI play a larger role in generating, optimizing, and applying regex patterns, developers can look forward to more powerful, efficient, and automated text manipulation capabilities. Regex will continue to be an essential tool in the Python ecosystem, and its integration with new technologies will open up exciting possibilities for the future.

In the coming years, we may even witness the emergence of hybrid systems that combine regex with AI-powered decision-making, allowing regex to be applied in more intuitive and context-sensitive ways. By mastering regex today, Python developers will be well-prepared to take full advantage of these future developments.

With this chapter, we have reached the end of our journey through the world of regular expressions in Python. From fundamental concepts to advanced use cases, we have equipped you with the knowledge and practical skills needed to use regex in a variety of real-world applications. As you continue to build your expertise in Python and regex, remember that mastering this tool is not only about writing complex patterns, but also about understanding how to use regex efficiently, maintainably, and creatively in solving text-processing challenges.

www.ingramcontent.com/pod-product-compliance
Lightning Source LLC
La Vergne TN
LVHW052058060326
832903LV00061B/3426